THE THREE CHAIRS
Experiencing Spiritual Breakthroughs

BRUCE H. WILKINSON

LifeWay Press
Nashville, Tennessee

ISBN 0-7673-9436-4

Dewey Decimal Classification: 248.82
Subject Heading: CHRISTIAN LIFE

This book is text for course CG-0524 in the subject area Personal Life
in the Christian Growth Study Plan.

Unless otherwise noted, Scripture quotations are from the Holy Bible, *New King James Version*,
copyright © 1979, 1980, 1982, Thomas Nelson, Inc., Publishers.

Order additional copies of *Three Chairs* resources by writing Customer Service Center, MSN 113;
127 Ninth Avenue, North; Nashville, TN 37234-0113; by calling toll free (800) 458-2772;
by faxing (615) 251-5933; by ordering online at *www.lifeway.com*;
by emailing *customerservice@lifeway.com*; or by visiting a LifeWay Christian Store.

For more information on adult discipleship and family resources, training, and events
check Web site *www.lifeway.com/discipleplus*.

Printed in the United States of America

LifeWay Press
127 Ninth Avenue, North
Nashville, Tennessee 37234

LifeWay

*As God works through us, we will help people and churches know
Jesus Christ and seek His Kingdom by providing biblical solutions that
spiritually transform individuals and cultures.*

CONTENTS

MEET BRUCE WILKINSON

Dr. Bruce H. Wilkinson is founder and president of Walk Thru the Bible Ministries, with headquarters in Atlanta, Georgia. Walk Thru the Bible is an international organization dedicated to ministering in over 75 countries and 50 languages and to providing the finest Bible teaching tools, and training. You may already be familiar with Bruce's work from such courses as *The 7 Laws of the Learner, Personal Holiness in Times of Temptation, The Biblical Portrait of Marriage, Walk Thru the Old Testament, Walk Thru the New Testament,* and publications such as *The Daily Walk, The Family Walk,* and *Youth Walk.*

You will find in *The Three Chairs: Experiencing Spiritual Breakthroughs* the same evidence of Christian commitment, calling, and quality of presentation and content. But you will also find a message that is very personal to you. This material speaks to you about your life and the life of your family—both those who have gone before you, laying the foundation for your faith, and those who will follow you, walking in your footsteps.

After a personal, startling experience in 1972, Bruce began to explore the Bible for evidence of a faith that passes from one generation to another. His testimony and his life shape these pages and guide you into a similar exploration of your own life and faith—one that can lead to spiritual breakthroughs.

Bruce graduated from Northeastern Bible College (B.A., 1969; Th.B., 1970), Dallas Theological Seminary (Th.M., 1974), and Western Seminary (D.D., 1988).

He and his wife, Darlene, have three children—David, Jennifer, and Jessica–and three grandchildren.

INTRODUCTION

Chairs. You probably have all different kinds in your house. You may have recliners, rockers, dining room or kitchen chairs, stools, wingbacks, folding chairs, director's chairs, beanbags, or office chairs. Depending on your family, you may also have high chairs, infant seats, or wheelchairs.

Just as the chairs you have in your home are personal to the tastes, comfort, size, and needs of your family, this book is designed for you to customize the material to meet your own needs. Some readers will go straight through the book, experiencing all four chapters. Some will study only two; others will work through three.

The first chapter is for everyone. In chapter 1, "Experiencing Spiritual Breakthroughs in Your Life," you will discover which "chair" you sit in and whether it is the chair you choose to continue to occupy. Whether you currently sit in the first, second, or third chair, you can experience personal, spiritual breakthroughs as you study this chapter.

Chapter 2, "Experiencing Spiritual Breakthroughs in Your Marriage," is targeted primarily to married couples, but is also an excellent study for engaged couples and young adults anticipating married life.

The third chapter, "Experiencing Spiritual Breakthroughs in Your Family," targets parents, especially with children who still live at home. This chapter is also excellent for couples planning to have children. And many adults with grown children and grandchildren will also benefit from studying this chapter.

The final chapter, "Experiencing Spiritual Breakthroughs with God," is for everyone and draws you to an even deeper relationship with Christ. Specific ideas are shared that provide wonderful tracks to deepen your walk with the Lord.

Now, find your favorite chair. Choose a place where you can read, write, and reflect on what God has done and is doing in your life. And experiencing spiritual breakthroughs with God.

CHAPTER 1

Experiencing Spiritual Breakthroughs in Your Life

VIEWER GUIDE

As you watch the video presentation, fill in the blanks in the statements.

Breakthrough: a sudden advance, especially in knowledge, insight, or experience

Breakthroughs from the Life of Joshua

(Josh. 24:14-15,31; Judg. 2:7,10)

The Three Generations of Joshua

- First Chair represents _Joshua_ .

- Second Chair represents the _Elders/children_

- Third Chair represents the next _generations after the elders_

Relationship to God

- First Chair _knew_ the Lord. (_saved_)

- Second Chair _knew_ the Lord.

- Third Chair _knew not_ the Lord.

The General Characteristic

- First Chair is a person of _Commitment_ .

- Second Chair is a person of _Compromise_ .

- Third Chair is a person of _Conflict_ .

The Works of God

- Joshua's generation _had_ the works.

- The elders _had seen_ the works.

- The next generation *did not know* the works.

Notes: _____

_____

_____

Breakthroughs from the Life of Abraham

The Three Generations of Abraham

- First Chair represents *Abraham*.

- Second Chair represents *Isaac*.

- Third Chair represents *Jacob*.

Relationship to God

- First Chair has a relationship of *God first / me*

- Second Chair has a relationship of *me / God*.

- Third Chair has a relationship of *me*.

The Word of God

- First Chair makes decisions based on *scripture*

- Second Chair makes decisions based on *saints*.

- Third Chair makes decisions based on *society*.

Notes: _____

_____

_____

_____

Breakthroughs from the Life of David

The Three Generations of David

- First Chair represents _David_
- Second Chair represents _Solomon_.
- Third Chair represents _Rehoboam_.

The Relationship to God

- First Chair has a _whole_ heart.
- Second Chair has a _half_ heart.
- Third Chair has _no_ heart.

The General Characteristic

- First Chair focuses on _people_.
- Second Chair focuses on _possessions_.
- Third Chair focuses on _purposelessness_.

Serving God

- First Chair wants to _serve God_.
- Second Chair wants to _satisfy self_.
- Third Chair wants to _seek peace_

Notes: _____

_____

_____

_____

_____

Breakthroughs from the Teachings of Paul

Insights from the apostle Paul

- First Chair is _spiritual_   *1 Cor: 2 + 3*
- Second Chair is _Carnal_.
- Third Chair is _natural_.

Breakthroughs from the Words of Christ
(Revelation 3:15-16,19)

The Observations of Christ

- First Chair is _hot_.
- Second Chair is _Lukewarm_.
- Third Chair is _Cold_.

Notes: _Rev. 3:19_ _____

_____

Hardest person to reach is the child of a second chair Christian

What Is Your Response?

- First Chair is invited to _Re-commit_ to Christ.
- Second Chair is invited to _repent_ before Christ. *V: 19*
- Third Chair is invited to _receive_ Christ.

WEEKLY STUDY

Key Verse
Choose for yourselves this day whom you will serve. ... But as for me and my house, we will serve the Lord (Josh. 24:15).

This Week's Study
Day 1: Lessons from the Life of Joshua
Day 2: Lessons from the Life of Abraham
Day 3: Lessons from the Life of David
Day 4: Lessons from the Teachings of Paul
Day 5: Lessons from the Words of Christ

Firsthand faith is a choice you make.

Remember the story of Goldilocks? When she visited the bears' home, she found three chairs. She tried all three and found that one of them fit her just right. Not everyone is comfortable in the same chair. Some are too hard; some are too soft; and some are just right.

Sometimes, however, we become too comfortable in our chairs, just as in our relationship with God through Jesus Christ. We may not have discovered the chair that is just right. As you study God's Word and reflect on the meanings of the three chairs, you may become increasingly uncomfortable in your chair and find that you would like to move.

The goal of this study is to show you what life in the first chair, representing firsthand faith, can offer. If you are already in this chair, you too will find spiritual breakthroughs as you seek an even closer walk with God.

Perhaps you will discover that you are in the second chair. You know you are a Christian, and you often go to church. You may not have realized that life with Christ could offer so much more. Exciting spiritual breakthroughs await you as you consider a move to the first chair.

Some of you will discover that you are sitting in the third chair. Because you did not experience the Word and works of God when you were growing up, you may never have taken that initial step of faith. You may discover for the first time the joy of knowing Jesus.

Each person who sits in the first chair has at some point made that choice. Although the home we grow up in greatly influences our relationship with Jesus Christ, becoming a Christian is an individual decision. Following that initial decision, the walk we have with Christ is also a choice we make. We can choose to make God the center of our lives; we can choose to keep him in the "Sunday" part of our lives; or we can choose to shut God out of our lives altogether. The choice is ours to make. We can benefit from our parents' and grandparents' faith experiences, but ultimately each of us must decide to follow Christ or go the world's way.

The Bible is full of models that will help us explore the meaning of each of the three chairs and the kind of faith they represent. With each example we will discover opportunities for a spiritual breakthrough.

Day 1: Lessons from the Life of Joshua

What can we do to ensure that our faith abides and flourishes in the next generation?

Scripture reveals the solution to this crucial issue of passing on our faith, and it paves the way for us to understand which things change from one generation to the next. More importantly, the Bible shows us what we can do about it.

Before we look at what the Bible says, let's review the meaning of the three chairs.

- The **first chair** in our metaphor is the godly chair, and those who sit in it remain close to Him.
- The **second chair** represents those who were raised in a firsthand faith family; they had the benefit of their parents' faith, and they accepted Christ as Savior in that environment. But for some reason they did not choose to stay close to God.
- The **third chair** is the godless chair, and those who sit in it have rejected God. They have moved away from Him, so as to focus on themselves. From godliness to godlessness—that's the general movement of history.

✳ **Place an X on the line where you believe you are right now.**
Godlessness   Godliness

Joshua is a primary example of a person who sits in the first chair. He knew the Lord and lived his life to serve Him. Even though others around him did not follow the Lord God, Joshua did. He took a public stand and followed God. Joshua also made a commitment that his family would follow God, too. (See Joshua 24:14-15.)

Joshua loved the Lord. He had a heart for God, and he committed his family to serve God. Joshua had firsthand faith. And his family daily witnessed a man totally committed to serving the Lord. Others of Joshua's generation had firsthand faith, too. They had seen God work mighty wonders; they knew that God had been with them during the difficult times of taking the promised land. This generation had firsthand knowledge and experience of God at work in their midst. People with firsthand faith, who sit in the first chair, know God, love God, and have personally experienced the mighty works of God.

But the elders who outlived Joshua did not have as close a walk with God. They chose the second chair. They knew about the mighty works of God and the faith of Joshua, but they had not experienced them at the same level for themselves. (See Joshua 24:31; Judges 2:7.)

Children who are raised by parents with firsthand faith see their parents' commitment, and they are aware of prayers God has answered. The overwhelming majority receive Jesus Christ as their personal Saviour but frequently never become as committed to Christ as their parents. They live under the power and influence of their parents' faith, but they never chose to move to the first chair. They are content to sit in the second chair and observe their parents' faith rather than move to the first chair and experience God's works for themselves.

Now therefore, fear the Lord, serve Him in sincerity and in truth, and put away the gods which your fathers served on the other side of the River and in Egypt. Serve the Lord! ... Choose for yourselves this day whom you will serve, whether the gods which your fathers served that were on the other side of the River, or the gods of the Amorites, in whose land you dwell. But as for me and my house, we will serve the Lord (Josh. 24:14-15).

Israel served the Lord all the days of Joshua, and all the days of the elders who outlived Joshua, who had known all the works of the Lord which He had done for Israel (Josh. 24:31).

So the people served the Lord all the days of Joshua, and all the days of the elders who outlived Joshua, who had seen all the great works of the Lord which He had done for Israel (Judg. 2:7).

When all that generation had been gathered to their fathers, another generation arose after them who did not know the Lord nor the work which He had done for Israel (Judg. 2:10).

The elders who followed Joshua sat in the second chair. The faith of their fathers had been enough to cause them to believe in God. They knew about the miracles of the parting of the Red Sea, how water had flowed from a rock, and how God had provided manna in the wilderness. They knew their parents had marched around the walls of Jericho. They believed all these acts of God, but they had not dedicated themselves to the Lord on the same "sold-out" level.

※ **Did you grow up in a family of faith? Can you recall family stories that led you to believe in God? Recall some faith stories from your childhood and briefly write about one of them below.**

_____

_____

_____

_____

Perhaps because the elders, content with second-chair living and secondhand faith, never actually experienced the works of God personally, the generations that followed occupied the third chair. They did not know God.

Because we have the Bible, we know the miraculous stories of how God worked in Joshua's generation. We may find it difficult to believe that just a couple of generations following Joshua's, the people didn't even know these stories. Why didn't they? Perhaps their parents never told them. When their parents told them stories about their grandparents, maybe the children asked about the parents' stories and about how God was working in their lives. The parents had no personal stories to tell. Over time they may have stopped telling the stories out of embarrassment for not having any miracles in their own lives.

The children of parents with second-chair faith do not see the works of God or hear about the works of God. They may see parents who go through the motions of faith—going to church on Sunday most of the time—but they don't see evidence of that faith in their parents' everyday lives. Instead of witnessing firsthand faith, they hear ancient stories that lead them to believe they are hearing about a dated, outmoded religion that cannot have meaning today in their own lives. They don't see enough to cause them to value the faith of their fathers, and so they choose not to believe. Ultimately the person in the third chair forsakes the Lord God of their fathers, does evil in the sight of the Lord, and replaces God with other gods.

Let's review the lessons we have learned from Joshua and following generations about their places in the three chairs.

- The first-chair person is saved.
- The second-chair person is saved.
- The third-chair person is not saved.

- The first-chair person has experienced the works of God.
- The second-chair person has heard about the works of God.
- The third-chair person doesn't know about the works of God.

One more way of looking at the three chairs is to consider their primary characteristics. The first-chair person is marked by a life of commitment. That is evident in Joshua's life. Joshua was wholeheartedly committed to serving the Lord.

The second chair is characterized by compromise. The person in this chair claims to love God and to follow His Word but often slowly moves away from God and lives a life distant from and not fully pleasing to God. The person in the second chair may go to church every Sunday, be a faithful member of the choir, and may even attend other church functions, but God generally has no part in the day-to-day life of a second-chair Christian. Second-chair Christians do not fully trust or obey God.

The third-chair person faces a life filled with conflict. When you grow up in a home that knows the Lord but doesn't honor Him as Lord, a home that compromises throughout life in many private and public ways, you can't help but be troubled by internal conflict. The people who occupy this chair serve the gods of society—personal desires, possessions, peer pressure, position.

※ **Which C characterizes your life? Circle the one that applies.**

Commitment   Compromise   Conflict

Three chairs are pictured on the next page. The one on the right is the first chair; the one on the left is the second chair; and the one in the back is the third chair. Where do you sit? Do you sit in the first chair, experiencing the presence of God and allowing Him to use you, shape you, and minister to others through you? Or do you sit in the second chair believing the truth and appreciating what God is doing in the lives of others but always wondering why you don't have the same spiritual passion they do? Or are you in the third chair, having never really accepted Christ as your personal Savior?

Then the children of Israel did evil in the sight of the Lord, and served the Baals; and they forsook the Lord God of their fathers (Judg. 2:11-12).

Commitment: an act of trust

Compromise: a blend of ideas of two different perspectives

Conflict: incompatibility; an antagonistic state

✹ **Write your name in the box beside the chair where you sit.**

The Third Chair
Knows not God
Knows not God's works
Serves false gods
No Faith

The Second Chair
Knows God
Knows about God's works
Serves the Lord of their fathers
Secondhand Faith

The First Chair
Knows God
Experiences God's works
Serves the Lord
Firsthand Faith

A Deeper Look
Joshua led the people of Israel into the Promised Land. He was God's chosen leader, and he walked with God daily.

✹ **Read the following passages in your Bible and list evidences of Joshua's walk with God.**

Numbers 13:1-2,16–14:9 _____

_____

Joshua 1:1-15 _____

_____

Joshua 3:1–4:8 _____

_____

Joshua 6:1-6,15-20 _____

_____

Joshua 23:1-3,6,8,11 _____

_____

Hold fast to the Lord your God (Josh. 23:8).

Are you satisfied with your walk with God? Pray that God will show you through the life of Joshua the ways you can have a spiritual breakthrough in your own life.

InterACTion

If your parents or grandparents modeled a first-chair faith for you, call or write them today if possible and thank them for the faith you saw in their lives. If they have gone to be with the Lord, voice a prayer of thanksgiving for their example of faith.

Day 2: Lessons from the Life of Abraham

How do you make decisions? Do you make them quickly without much thought, or is decision-making difficult for you? Do you ask for help and consider the advice of friends? Do you read God's Word to find an answer and seek God's help through prayer?

Honor: to treat with respect; to live up to terms of commitment

People with firsthand faith honor the Bible. They read it regularly. They meditate on God's Word. They talk with God throughout the day.

☀ Do you identify with one of the stories below? Write your name in the blank at the beginning of the appropriate story.

_____ begins the day with a quiet time. Facing the day without spending time alone with God would be a major disappointment, and rarely happens. Reading the Bible and talking with God is a part of daily life.

_____ races out the door late on Sunday because the Bible is missing again. Never could find it. Just have to go to church without it this week. Wait, look, there it is on the backseat. Great! Having your own Bible at church is important.

_____ thinks there's a Bible in the house somewhere. Yeah, the one that belonged to Grandmother. Is it on the shelf? or in that box of old books in the garage? or did it just disappear?

Abraham had firsthand faith. He made decisions based on what God told him to do. Even if he didn't understand God's direction, he trusted God to guide him.

15

Abram believed the Lord, and he credited it to him as righteousness (Gen. 15:6).

Each chair represents a different attitude toward God:
1st Chair: God and me
       (Abraham)
2nd Chair: Me and God
       (Isaac)
3rd Chair: Me (Jacob)

"I will bless you, and multiplying I will multiply your descendants as the stars of the heaven and as the sand which is on the seashore; and your descendants shall possess the gate of their enemies. In your seed all the nations of the earth shall be blessed, because you have obeyed My voice" *(Gen. 22: 17-18).*

✷ Remember when God told Abraham to sacrifice his son Isaac? Read Genesis 22:1-18 in your Bible. What evidence do you see that Abraham put God first in his life?

_____

_____

_____

_____

By the time we get to Jacob, we find a man who no longer puts God first. Indeed most of his life, Jacob put himself first. Jacob exhibited characteristics of a person in the third chair.

✷ Check and read one or more of the following passages:

☐ Genesis 25:27-34   ☐ Genesis 27:1-38   ☐ Genesis 31:17-21

What evidence do you see that Jacob put himself first?

_____

_____

_____

_____

People in each of the three chairs relate in a different way to God and to one another. Consider these differences.

People with firsthand faith have a relationship with God, a daily walk that shapes who they are and what they do. Because of that relationship, they rely on God's Word to guide them. Theirs is not a time-of-crisis religion. God is with them in crisis because they are with God every day.

People with secondhand faith know that their parents put God first. On Saturday night they saw their parents prepare for Sunday morning. Perhaps lying together on the hall table were their parent's Sunday School books, their well-worn Bibles, and their offering envelopes holding a check for their offering to the Lord.

But people in the second chair don't have time to meet God daily in a quiet place. They have too many personal desires to give that much money to the church; after all, who knows what they give anyway as long as they are seen giving something. It seems only natural to put themselves first. God still has a corner of their lives but not the central place. Going to church has become a responsibility; they have no joy because they are not in a close relationship with God. They admit that sometimes they do hear good words of wisdom from the saints at the church. Some of that advice sounds pretty good, but they seldom recall it on Monday. Unless, of course, they also do business with those same church members.

Understandably, many people who grow up in a household with second-chair parents like those described above won't see much reason to put God first or to go to church. They often see their parents as hypocrites and assume the church is full of people just like them. With that kind of perception, they see God as only the symbol of religion, something they don't have time to include in their busy lives.

Relationship: a connection that binds participants

Responsibility: a duty, burden, or obligation.

Religion: an institutional system of attitudes, beliefs, and practices

If you earnestly obey My commandments which I command you today, to love the Lord your God and serve Him with all your heart and with all your soul, then I will give you the rain for your land in its season, the early rain and the latter rain, that you may gather in your grain, your new wine, and your oil. And I will send grass in your fields for your livestock, that you may eat and be filled (Deut. 11:13-15).

❋ **Which word describes your walk with God? Check one box.**

☐ relationship ☐ responsibility ☐ religion

❋ **Which phrase best fits your value system? Check one box.**

☐ God and me ☐ me and God ☐ me

❋ **Where do you search for answers about life's questions?**

☐ Scripture ☐ saints ☐ society

❋ **Remember the dramatic vignette on the video? Describe evidences that the grandfather, Harrison Taylor, had a firsthand faith. Describe how you know his son, Stephen, had a secondhand faith.**

_____

_____

_____

_____

A Deeper Look
After Jacob left the home of Laban, his father-in-law, he turned toward home, to face Esau again.

✳ **Read Genesis 32:3–33:18 in your Bible. Did Jacob move to the first chair as a result of this journey?** ☐ Yes ☐ No ☐ Maybe **Do you see any evidence that he changed from putting himself first to putting God first?**

_____

_____

_____

Do you need to move from the chair you are in? Pray for insights into how you can experience spiritual breakthroughs that result in a closer walk with God.

InterACTion

If you were to put the Lord first in your life and live in the first chair, what changes would you have to make? How would being sold out to God alter the way you live on a daily basis? Would the people close to you recognize a difference?

Day 3: Lessons from the Life of David

Blessed are the undefiled in the way, Who walk in the law of the Lord! Blessed are those who keep His testimonies, Who seek Him with the whole heart! (Ps. 119:1-2).

Wholehearted: completely and sincerely devoted, determined, enthusiastic

The picture is becoming increasingly clear. People who sit in the first chair have a wholehearted love relationship with God the Father through their Savior Jesus Christ. Today we're going to look at the life of David who was called "a man after [God's] own heart" (1 Sam. 13:14). David is a good example at this point because his life shows that in spite of tragic mistakes and times of sin he had a firsthand faith with God.

The Bible is full of evidence that David had a heart devoted to God. Let's look at some examples.

God told Samuel to choose David as the next king of Israel, succeeding Saul. Even though David was only a young boy at the time, God said to Samuel, "Do not look at his appearance or at his physical stature … For the Lord does not see as man sees; for man looks at the outward appearance, but the Lord looks at the heart" (1 Sam. 16:7).

Even as a young man, David walked with God. When he offered to face Goliath, he said, "The Lord, who delivered me from the paw of the lion and from the paw of the bear, He will deliver me from the hand of this Philistine" (1 Sam. 17:37).

David was God's chosen king. One of his actions was to bring the ark of the covenant to Jerusalem. Read about David's worship in

1 Chronicles 16:1-3. David loved God, and he cared about God's people. For worship that day David wrote a psalm of thanksgiving, and the people worshiped God with the sound of the trumpets.

David sought to pass on his faith to his son Solomon, the son who inherited his throne. His instructions to Solomon included these words:

> As for you, my son Solomon, know the God of your father, and serve Him with a loyal heart and with a willing mind; for the Lord searches all hearts and understands all the intent of the thoughts. If you seek Him, He will be found by you; but if you forsake Him, He will cast you off forever (1 Chron. 28:9).

David was both king and songwriter. He wrote many of the psalms. Here are a few familiar verses that reflect David's heart for God.

> I will praise You, O Lord, with my whole heart;
> I will tell of all Your marvelous works.
> I will be glad and rejoice in You;
> I will sing praise to Your name, O Most High (Ps. 9:1-2).

> Let the words of my mouth and the meditation of my heart
> Be acceptable in Your sight,
> O Lord, my strength and my Redeemer (Ps. 19:14).

> He who has clean hands and a pure heart,
> Who has not lifted up his soul to an idol,
> Nor sworn deceitfully.
> He shall receive blessing from the Lord,
> And righteousness from the God of his salvation (Ps. 24:4-5).

Choose one of these verses. Write it on a card and carry it with you this week. Commit it to memory.

Solomon knew David's heart. He knew that his father had wanted to build a temple for God, but God allowed Solomon to build the temple. Yes, Solomon knew God, but did he make Him Lord of his life? Look at this passage in 1 Kings 11 describing Solomon later in life.

> For it was so, when Solomon was old, that ... his heart was not loyal to the Lord his God, as was the heart of his father David. For Solomon went after Ashtoreth the goddess of the Sidonians, and after Milcom the abomination of the Ammonites. Solomon did evil in the sight of the Lord, and did not fully follow the Lord, as did his father David. ... So

So they brought the ark of God, and set it in the midst of the tabernacle that David had erected for it. Then they offered burnt offerings and peace offerings before God. And when David had finished offering the burnt offerings and the peace offerings, he blessed the people in the name of the Lord. Then he distributed to everyone of Israel, both man and woman, to everyone a loaf of bread, a piece of meat, and a cake of raisins (1 Chron. 16:1-3).

Halfhearted: lacking spirit or interest

the Lord became angry with Solomon, because his heart had turned from the Lord God of Israel (1 Kings 11:4-6,9).

Solomon served God with half a heart.

What could have turned Solomon's heart away from God? The Bible tells us that Solomon was very wealthy. Perhaps he began to take more pleasure in his possessions than he did in following God and ruling the people with love.

✳ Read Deuteronomy 17:14-20 in your Bible. List three things God told the kings of Israel not to do.

1. _____

2. _____

3. _____

Now read about Solomon's wealth in 1 Kings 4:26 and 11:1-3. In what ways did Solomon's lifestyle violate God's Law?

_____

_____

_____

_____

If David had a heart for God, and Solomon had half a heart for God, Rehoboam had no heart for God. Rehoboam was Solomon's son and his successor to the throne. He obviously grew up as a privileged person. Rehoboam had everything he could desire in the way of material wealth. He was a world leader and knew other world leaders. But Rehoboam grew up in a home of secondhand faith, and he hardened his heart against God.

Rehoboam quickly turned from the godly characteristics of David. David cared about his people, planned a Holy City for them, and planned feast days for them. Soon after Rehoboam succeeded Solomon, he was faced with a decision.

✳ Read 2 Chronicles 10:1-14 in your Bible. What did Rehoboam do?

_____

To whom did he listen? _____

Was this what God wanted him to do?   ☐ Yes ☐ No

✳ Read 2 Chronicles 12:1. How would you describe the reign of Rehoboam?

_____

And you will seek Me and find Me, when you search for Me with all your heart (Jer. 29:13).

✳ David, Solomon, and Rehoboam each had a different focus in life. Draw a line to match the man with the focal pattern of his life.

David   •   • purposelessness

Solomon   •   • possessions

Rehoboam •   • people

We live in a materialistic age. For many people shopping malls have replaced the church as the center of their lives. They go there to meet people, to find out what's new, to try to fill the emptiness in their lives. One wealthy man is quoted as saying, "Shortly after I realized I had plenty, I discovered there was plenty more."

How much is enough? Are possessions the most important thing in your life? David wrote, "May He grant you according to your heart's desire, and fulfill all your purpose" (Ps. 20:4). If God granted you the desire of your heart, what would you receive?

✳ Draw a heart around the answer that honestly represents your heart's desire.

to acquire possessions	to enjoy personal pleasure
to attain power and prestige	to love God and serve people

Delight yourself also in the Lord, And He shall give you the desires of your heart. Commit your way to the Lord, Trust also in Him, And He shall bring it to pass (Ps. 37:4-5).

How does your choice reflect your walk with God (the chair in which you sit)?

_____

_____

Create in me a clean heart,
O God,
And renew a steadfast spirit
within me (Ps. 51:10).

But seek first the kingdom of
God and His righteousness,
and all these things shall be
added to you (Matt. 6:33).

A Deeper Look

Complete the chart below to determine how you spend your time and money. This will indicate your priorities. Estimate how you have spent your time in the past week and your money in the past month.

My Life	% of time to achieve	% of money to achieve
Possessions	_____	_____
Pleasure	_____	_____
Power/Prestige	_____	_____
People	_____	_____

Pray that God will give you a spiritual breakthrough that you will have a heart for God.

InterACTion

If possessions have been your god, call a welfare agency in your area and ask them what they need. Take steps to meet that need by sending a check or providing what they need. Or volunteer in a nonprofit organization to help those less fortunate than you. Reverse the possessions-over-people trend by putting people first and possessions last. What a difference it will make in how you approach life.

Day 4: Lessons from the Teachings of Paul

Images of firsthand faith, secondhand faith, and lack of faith—first-chair Christians, second-chair Christians, and third-chair non-Christians—are not limited to the Old Testament. The study for today and tomorrow focuses on New Testament examples.

All that could be said of a person in the first chair in the Old Testament can be said of a first-chair Christian in the New Testament. Look at the life of Paul, for example. Paul, like Joshua, knew the Lord personally. In fact, he called himself an apostle because he had personally encountered Christ on the Damascus road. His life was wholly committed to telling the good news about Jesus Christ. And throughout his missionary journeys, he experienced the mighty works of God. Like Abraham, he put God first, and his relationship with God mattered most to him. He trusted the Word of God and used it to tell how Jesus was the fulfillment of the Old Testament prophesies. Like David he gave his whole heart to his ministry of reaching people.

✹ Whom do you know who models, as Paul did, a dynamic first-hand faith? Perhaps a parent, a minister, or someone else who has modeled the first-chair Christian for you. Using the following words from the previous paragraph, describe that person.

knew	commitment	experienced	whole
first	relationship	Word	people

_____

_____

_____

_____

_____

What things were gain to me, these I have counted loss for Christ (Phil. 3:7).

For God so loved the world that He gave His only begotten Son, that whoever believes in Him should not perish but have everlasting life. For God did not send His Son into the world to condemn the world, but that the world through Him might be saved (John 3:16-17).

The greatest of these is love (1 Cor. 13:13).

I can do all things through Christ who strengthens me (Phil. 4:13).

Paul's humble service clearly gives evidence of his commitment to people—to those Jesus came to save. While in constant personal danger and risk of bodily harm and imprisonment, Paul continued to tell people about Christ.

Contemporary Christians are indebted to Paul for the model he gave and for the letters he wrote to New Testament churches. Paul taught both by example and through his letters how we should live as Christians. As he modeled a sacrificial life of love for people, he also wrote about it.

✹ Read 1 Corinthians 13. Draw a symbol to represent what Paul said was the most important spiritual gift.

Paul's letters were written to encourage Christians, like Timothy, and to strengthen struggling churches such as those at Ephesus, Philippi, and Corinth. The individuals and churches shared Paul's letters, extending his love and encouragement so that many were blessed.

✻ Look at the chart below. Honestly evaluate your love for those for whom Christ died. Check the appropriate columns.

	Rarely	Sometimes	Usually	Frequently	Fervently
I love people					
I serve people					
I pray for people					

✻ In which area would you most like to improve. Write a prayer in the space below expressing your desire for a breakthrough in increasing your love for people.

_____

_____

_____

_____

Paul offered a specific example that parallels the concept of the three chairs. In writing to the church at Corinth, Paul addressed disagreements and divisions among the people there. Paul was grieved to hear about their inability to get along with one another, the superior attitude of some believers, and the immorality among some.

In 1 Corinthians 2:9-12, Paul described the spiritual person, the first-chair believer, the mature Christian. This believer's wisdom comes from God. Through the Holy Spirit the spiritual person discerns "the things of God" (1 Cor. 2:11). The Holy Spirit reveals to the spiritual person "the things that have been freely given to us by God" (1 Cor. 2:12). Through a close relationship with God, we increase our appreciation for all the good gifts God has given us.

But many of the people in Corinth were not "spiritual"; they were "carnal"—babes in Christ. They were Christians but had grown very little. They were not "sold out" to God. They were sitting in the second chair. Paul said that among this group in the church was "envy, strife, and divisions" (1 Cor. 3:3).

Some were bragging about following Paul or Apollos; all should have been humbly following the living Christ! Paul told them that whoever had led them to Christ did nothing; the Spirit of God did everything.

Who then is Paul, and who is Apollos, but ministers through whom you believed, as the Lord gave to each one? I planted, Apollos watered, but God gave the increase. So then neither he who plants is anything, nor he who waters, but God who gives the increase. ...For we are God's fellow workers; you are God's field, you are God's building. According to the grace of God which was given to me, as a wise master builder I have laid the foundation, and another builds on it. But let each one take heed how he builds on it. For no other foundation can anyone lay than that which is laid, which is Jesus Christ (1 Cor. 3:5-7,9-11).

Paul also spoke of the "natural" person, the one occupying the third chair: "The natural man does not receive the things of the Spirit of God, for they are foolishness to him; nor can he know them, because they are spiritually discerned" (1 Cor. 2:14). The natural man doesn't know God; and because he does not have the discernment of the Holy Spirit, he can understand nothing about spiritual matters until he first accepts Christ as Savior.

Who gets the credit? Is it important to you to receive public acclaim for the ways you support your church? Do you pray like the Pharisee or the humble tax collector (see Luke 18:10-14)? Do you do good deeds just so you can tell someone about them next week? Do you visit the hospital so you can give a public report, calling attention to yourself?

※ **When is the last time you secretly ministered in Christ's name? Note that good deed in the space below.**

_____

_____

A Deeper Look
One of the meanings of the word carnal relates to the temporal. When second-chair Christians put themselves before God, they are making the temporal more important than the eternal.

※ **What temptations do you face in putting worldly, temporary pleasures and feelings ahead of eternal truths? Write one below.**

_____

Pray that God will help you resist temptation and help you stay focused on Him as you "press toward the goal for the prize of the upward call of God in Christ Jesus" (Phil. 3:14).

Spiritual: relating to sacred matters

Carnal: relating to temporal, bodily pleasures

Natural: conforming to human reason alone

Do not lay up for yourselves treasures on earth, where moth and rust destroy and where thieves break in and steal; but lay up for yourselves treasures in heaven, where neither moth nor rust destroys and where thieves do not break in and steal. For where your treasure is, there your heart will be also (Matt. 6:19-21).

Temporal: relating to earthly life

Eternal: lasting forever

Roman Road

Step 1: Romans 3:23: "For all have sinned and fall short of the glory of God."

Step 2: Romans 6:23: "For the wages of sin is death, but the gift of God is eternal life in Christ Jesus our Lord."

Step 3: Romans 5:8: "But God demonstrates His own love toward us, in that while we were still sinners, Christ died for us."

Step 4: Romans 10:9-10: "If you confess with your mouth the Lord Jesus and believe in your heart that God has raised Him from the dead, you will be saved. For with the heart one believes unto righteousness, and with the mouth confession is made unto salvation."

InterACTion

Perhaps one of the temporal feelings you have is fear. Paul wrote to Timothy, "For God has not given us a spirit of fear, but of power and of love and of a sound mind" (2 Tim. 1:7).

✳ **You may want to share your faith but you have been afraid to do so. In the space below, express your fears or other reasons you do not freely share your personal testimony with those who do not know God.**

_____

_____

✳ **Write the names of three persons you know are sitting in the third chair, persons with whom you would like to share your faith.**

1. _____

2. _____

3. _____

✳ **Consider the eternal consequences if you let your fear control you. What might happen?**

_____

_____

One plan you can use to tell others about Christ came from Paul's letter to the Romans. It's called the Roman Road to salvation (see margin). Mark your New Testament so that you can quickly find these four verses. Practice telling your own salvation story and what God is doing in your life today. If you have had spiritual breakthroughs this week, include them in your testimony.

Now call someone you know is sitting in the third-chair and schedule a time to tell them about Christ. Begin now to pray about your visit. God will help you overcome your fear. The consequences are eternal.

Day 5: Lessons from the Words of Christ

All week you have considered biblical models that help expand the concept of the three chairs such as Old Testament examples of different groups or families: Joshua, the elders, and a later generation; Abraham, Isaac, and Jacob; David, Solomon, and Rehoboam. Then in the New Testament, the words of Paul gave even more meaning to the differences in people who have firsthand faith, secondhand faith, or no faith at all.

Today's study focuses on the words of Jesus, which contain the supreme example for Christians to follow. The words to consider, in light of the three chairs, come from the last book of the Bible, John's Revelation. The words were introduced in the video presentation. They are hot, cold, and lukewarm.

Hot describes the person in the first chair—one on fire for Jesus Christ. *Cold* refers to the person in the third chair, the one who does not know Jesus as Savior and Lord, has no faith, has no relationship to Him, and is cold to the things of God. And *lukewarm* refers to the person in the middle—one who is neither on fire for God nor unknown to God. *Lukewarm* sounds like a person who can't quite decide whether to be hot or cold, so he just straddles the line trying to make it both in the Christian world and the secular world.

Look at what Jesus said in Revelation 3:15 to those in the church at Laodicea: "I know your works, that you are neither cold nor hot. I could wish you were cold or hot. So then, because you are lukewarm, and neither cold nor hot, I will vomit you out of My mouth."

Jesus clearly didn't like the fence-straddling approach. The hot one is on fire for Jesus, and the cold one is more open to the gospel than the lukewarm person. Read on to see what else He had to say.

> Because you say, "I am rich, have become wealthy, and have need of nothing"—and do not know that you are wretched, miserable, poor, blind, and naked—I counsel you to buy from Me gold refined in the fire, that you may be rich; and white garments, that you may be clothed, that the shame of your nakedness may not be revealed; and anoint your eyes with eye salve, that you may see (Rev. 3:17-18).

This is not the first time the Bible has mentioned wealth as an obstacle to a close walk with God. This verse seems to indicate that people who have all they need, want, or desire physically are in special danger of becoming content, complacent, or perhaps lukewarm. And, somehow, they begin to think that the wealth and status they have attained are the result of their work, intelligence, or good fortune. They seem to forget to thank God for their ability to work, their good mind,

He who loves silver will not be satisfied with silver;
Nor he who loves abundance, with increase.
This also is vanity (Eccl. 5:10).

For the love of money is a root of all kinds of evil, for which some have strayed from the faith in their greediness, and pierced themselves through with many sorrows (1 Tim. 6:10).

No one can serve two masters; for either he will hate the one and love the other, or else he will be loyal to the one and despise the other. You cannot serve God and mammon (Matt. 6:24).

Mammon: material wealth or possessions

It is easier for a camel to go through the eye of a needle than for a rich man to enter the kingdom of God (Matt. 19:24).

But seek the kingdom of God, and all these things shall be added to you (Luke 12:31).

their skills, or their health; and often they fail to return to God an offering proportionate to His Divine blessing. They also fool themselves into thinking that material goods are the real way to measure wealth. Jesus said they do not have clear vision.

※ Jesus often spoke in parables. Read His parable in your Bible in Luke 12:16-21. What do you think the parable means?

_____

_____

_____

Now read about the rich young ruler in Matthew 19:16-22. What answer do you think the young man anticipated when he asked, "What do I still lack?"

_____

Jesus told him to do two things. What were they?

_____

_____

Why was the young man sorrowful?

_____

_____

Americans are wealthy. Yes, there are many poor people living in the United States; but by the world's standards, Americans are wealthy. We consume far more of the world's goods than other countries.

※ Read the items below. Check any that apply to you.
- ☐ I go shopping to forget my troubles.
- ☐ Buying a new (dress, golf club, computer software, pair of shoes, etc.) makes me feel good.
- ☐ My closet is so full I can never find what I want to wear.
- ☐ I packed some things to give to charity this week. I found things I had never worn before.

☐ I like to drive the newest car; I trade every year.

☐ We had to have a bigger house; the old one just got too crowded with all the furniture and things.

☐ We need a bigger car. The old one couldn't pull the new boat.

☐ We went on a trip overseas. We really bought some great stuff.

☐ I can't afford to give much of my money to the church. There are too many things I need before I can think about that!

☐ My credit cards are maxed out. I need another one.

☐ My neighbors just (landscaped their yard, put in a pool, added outdoor lighting, etc.); I guess I'll have to do the same.

☐ I just bought a new (VCR, computer, bread maker, hand-held computer, cell phone, etc.). I hope I can learn to use it.

Why are material possessions such a threat to our walk with God? Remember the first commandment? Look at Exodus 20:2-3: "I am the Lord your God....You shall have no other gods before Me." Maybe it is easier for a person with a lot of material goods to put "things" before God. Then things become our god because they get more attention than God does.

When we looked at the lives of Abraham, Isaac, and Jacob, we considered the different relationships people in the three chairs have with God: God and me, me and God, and me. Putting things before God is definitely putting me first.

When we looked at lessons from Paul, we considered the difference between temporal and eternal. Putting things before God is definitely a temporal value. In fact, Americans rarely hold on to anything anymore. Goods are more and more temporary. Have you tried to get an appliance repaired lately? The prevailing thought is to replace, not repair. We buy more and more and keep it for less and less time. In many ways, over and over again, the Bible warns about wealth.

※ Summarize these lessons on wealth in the space below. How do they apply to you?

_____

_____

Let's return to Revelation. Even though Jesus does not like a lukewarm church, He does not disown or destroy it. In Revelation 3:19-20, Jesus says, "As many as I love, I rebuke and chasten. Therefore be zealous and repent. Behold, I stand at the door and knock. If anyone hears My voice and opens the door, I will come in to him and dine with him, and he with Me."

Rebuke: to reprimand

Repent: to turn from sin and dedicate oneself to new behavior

Recommit: to once again give control to another

What does Jesus do? Jesus rebukes His own who stray from Him. Why does He do this? Just as a parent loves a child and out of love disciplines the child so that no harm will come to him, so our Heavenly Father rebukes those He loves and calls His children back to Him. Indeed, God does not discipline those who are "cold," those in the third chair; for they do not know Him or call Him Father or Lord.

Consider for a moment the image of the door and Jesus standing there knocking. In a famous painting of Jesus knocking at the door, the outsider has no way to open it. The popular interpretation is that Jesus waits at our heart's door for us to invite Him in. Generally we think of this as those without Christ who must open the door to receive Christ as Savior.

But that's not the case in the Revelation passage. Jesus is talking about those who are already Christians, even though they are lukewarm. What does Jesus say will happen if we open the door and let Him in? We'll have a closer fellowship with Him. It will be as intimate as friends sharing dinner together in one person's home—a close, warm, caring relationship.

If you are not currently enjoying that kind of close walk with God, what will you do? You can have a spiritual breakthrough. You can move from the overstuffed comfort of the easy chair in the middle to the love seat on the right where you can join Jesus in the first chair. If you want to open that door to a closer relationship with Jesus Christ, repent of placing other gods before Him, and recommit your life to following Him. Pray for His forgiveness, for the strength and courage to overcome obstacles in your walk with Christ, and for a desire for eternal values.

A Deeper Look

Do you believe entire institutions, such as Christian colleges, para-church ministries, or mission organizations, can find themselves in the first, second, or third chair with a firsthand relationship with God, a secondhand faith, or even no faith at all?

Review the applications from this week and relate them to churches rather than individuals. Consider the following questions.

- Does the church love people? or does the building come first?
- Do people bring and use their Bibles? or do they just listen as someone else reads?
- Is stewardship a priority?
- Does the church share its wealth with those outside the church in missions projects, feeding the hungry, helping the needy, and winning the lost?
- Do Sunday School classes study the Bible or something else?
- What's more important, the Ten Commandments or the church constitution and bylaws?

- Are there more Bibles than umbrellas in the church's lost and found?
- Does the Bible or society have more influence?
- Are people being won to Christ?
- How many people has the church baptized in the past year?
- Is the greater emphasis on fellowship or evangelism?

✳ In the space below describe a church with firsthand faith and then one with secondhand faith.

Firsthand faith church: _____

_____

_____

Secondhand faith church: _____

_____

_____

"Silver and gold I do not have, but what I do have I give you: In the name of Jesus Christ of Nazareth, rise up and walk." And he took him by the right hand and lifted him up, and immediately his feet and ankle bones received strength. So he, leaping up, stood and walked and entered the temple with them—walking, leaping, and praising God (Acts 3:6-8).

InterACTion
✳ Have you been in the second chair, straddling the space between the first and second chair, or allowing material possessions to interfere in your walk with God? If so, you may choose to repent and recommit your life to a closer walk with Christ, then list below specific steps you will take to honor that commitment and a date for beginning each action.

Action   Date

1. _____   _____

2. _____   _____

3. _____   _____

4. _____   _____

Spiritual Breakthroughs I Experienced in My Life This Week

CHAPTER 3

Experiencing Spiritual Breakthroughs in Your Marriage

VIEWER GUIDE

As you watch the video presentation, fill in the blanks in the statements.

First Chair spouses have a heart of marital *loyalty*.

Second Chair spouses have a heart of marital *treachery*.

Malachi 2: 13-14

NEVER, NEVER BOX
HOPE NOT BOX
PROBABLY NOT BOX
MAYBE NOT BOX
PROBABLY WILL BOX
HOPE TO BOX
SEVER, SEVER BOX

you break the covenant you made –

Guard: to tend to carefully

Breakthrough 1: Guard Your Marital Relationship
(Eph. 5:23; 1 Cor. 11:3, 8-9; Gen. 2:18)

Commit your marital _____ to be completely _____.

- The husband's role is to be the *head of his wife*.

- A First Chair husband must *lead –* (*not passive*)

- The wife's role is to be the (*submissive*) *helper*

- A First Chair wife lives to help her *husband*.

What kind of help does he need?

32

Notes: *Womans deepest need is*
security.
Mans deepest need is
significance.

Breakthrough 2: Fulfill Your Marital Roles
(Eph. 5:22-25)

Fulfill your biblical *responsibility* of Head and Helper.

- A husband's responsibility is to ___*love*___ his wife.

- A First Chair husband must love his wife *at all Times*

- A wife's responsibility is to ___*submit*___ to her husband.

- A First Chair wife must submit to her husband *in everything*

Notes: *no time in your marriage are*
you not to submit –

Breakthrough 3: Obey Your Marital Responsibilities

Obey your biblical *responsibilities* to love and submit.

Notes: _____

_____

_____

_____

_____

WEEKLY STUDY

Key Verse

Therefore a man shall leave his father and mother and be joined to his wife, and they shall become one flesh (Gen. 2:24).

This Week's Study

Day 1: Husbands and Wives: Guard Your Marital Relationship

Day 2: Husbands: Fulfill Your Marital Role

Day 3: Wives: Fulfill Your Marital Role

Day 4: Husbands: Fulfill Your Marital Responsibility

Day 5: Wives: Fulfill Your Marital Responsibility

Perhaps you have experienced building your own home. The steps are many. Where did you begin? You may have begun by trying to find just the right piece of property. You may have decided to choose your plans or hire someone to design a house just for you. But before the actual building could begin, you would want to hire someone to be in charge of the construction—someone you could trust, someone who would have your best interests in mind throughout the project, someone who would build that house as if you were going to live there for a lifetime.

Building a marriage is much the same. You may have known since you were a child that you wanted to be married someday. You may have thought about the person you would marry, the kind of wedding you would have, the kind of home you would share, the children you would raise. As you dreamed about your marriage, did you also think about who could help you have the best marriage possible, who would have your best interests at heart, who would expect you to live with your spouse for a lifetime? You may have had your parents to support you, but someone more qualified, more caring, more able to guide and bless your marriage is God.

If you build a house and the land is a poor choice, it may flood, or sink, or become damaged in a mud slide. If your builder is poorly equipped, your house may have flaws that cannot be fixed. In extreme cases, your house may be beyond repair.

The good news is that at whatever stage you are in your marriage, you can experience spiritual breakthroughs. If you listen and obey the Word of God, you can enjoy a marriage that is all you ever desired; and God will pour out his blessings on your marital relationship.

Whether you are still anticipating meeting your future spouse—you are engaged or a newlywed—or you've been married many years, you can have spiritual breakthroughs in your marriage. Whether you believe your marriage is currently in serious trouble or you find constant fulfillment and joy in your spouse, you can have a better marriage. You can have breakthroughs in the areas of relationships, roles, and responsibilities.

Day 1: Husbands and Wives— Guard Your Marital Relationship

When children look for a model for marriage, the one they know best is the relationship of their parents. Since many children today grow up in single-parent homes or blended homes, they may know little that is good about their parent's marriage. But their parents' model may still be the most familiar to them.

Last week we learned that, while each person must make an individual faith commitment, children are greatly influenced by the faith of their families. The home in which people grow up also affects their view of marriage. Some children grow up thinking they want a marriage just like their parents; others grow up thinking that if marriage is like their parents' they want no part in it!

✳ **How has your view of marriage been shaped by your parents' example? Give three examples in the space below.**

1. _____

2. _____

3. _____

Most of the time, as we have more experiences with other families, we learn that not all marriages are like our parents'.

✳ **If you could have a marriage like any couple you know, the best example you can recall, who would that model be? In the space below write their names and the reasons you believe they have a good marriage.**

_____

_____

_____

_____

The union of one man and one woman for life, the institution of marriage and the family, was one of the first events that happened after creation. Marriage and the family have been around for a long time. Good marriages and bad marriages have occurred throughout the centuries. Yet the basis for a good marriage never really changes. Through the Bible God provided some guidelines for a happy, holy marriage. This week's study will help you discover ways you can have spiritual breakthroughs to a godly marriage.

Even before you marry, your relationship to your spouse is very important. Loyalty is essential. And the closer you get to saying, "I do," the more important and essential that loyalty becomes. The first thing many people think about in loyalty is being faithful in a sexual union. That is, of course, essential, but loyalty means much more than that.

A first-chair marriage is marked by loyalty ...
• **mental loyalty**
• **emotional loyalty**
• **physical loyalty**
• **volitional loyalty**
• **unconditional loyalty**

Loyalty: being faithful and devoted to another

Let's explore the various dynamics of loyalty in a marriage relationship. Guarding your marital relationship is first a mental choice. Each person starts at the beginning of a relationship with a commitment to remain faithful. That commitment to remain forever faithful should be a promise that is never broken. That decision should not be based on how you feel that day or whether your spouse hurt your feelings or you had a disagreement. Your part of the marriage contract is to be faithful, and that is a mental choice. Once made, you may have to remind yourself and renew your pledge often, but it is a decision never to be broken.

In addition to thinking of first- and second-chair marriages, we can also think of boxes in which we place ourselves. We alone determine the box we're in, just as we decide which chair we will occupy in our walk with God.

The first box is the "never, never box." That's the first-chair box. The person in this box has made a firm commitment that the most important earthly relationship is to one's spouse and that relationship demands loyalty. The marriage partner in the never, never box has promised to remain forever faithful, regardless of what the marriage brings—sickness, unemployment, hardships, even an unfaithful spouse. The choice to stay in the never, never box is a personal decision, made apart from any action of the spouse.

NEVER, NEVER BOX

The second box is the "hope not box." You "hope" you will remain faithful, but sometimes you daydream about what life with another partner might be like. You see another person and you wonder *What if...* Allowing the daydream to begin and grow is one step out of the never, never box. It represents the first tiny crack in the marriage relationship.

HOPE NOT BOX

The third box is the "probably not box." You think you probably won't be unfaithful. But still your mind begins to think about how attractive someone else is and to appreciate the attention someone else offers. After all, sometimes that other person seems to be more attentive than your spouse. Such thoughts move one further away from the never, never box.

PROBABLY NOT BOX

The fourth box, the box in the middle, is the "maybe crisis box." The person in this box is just as likely to move toward a loyal relationship with the spouse as to unfaithfulness. The danger of disloyalty is ever increasing.

MAYBE CRISIS BOX

The fifth box is the "probably will box." The likelihood is increasing that marriage vows will be broken. The marriage may not last. You may begin to share conversations with another that once were and still should be reserved only for your spouse. You are being mentally disloyal to your spouse, perhaps sharing disagreements or difficulties known only to the two of you. You are seriously looking around.

PROBABLY WILL BOX

The sixth box is the "hope to box." By now you have decided that the marriage is a lost cause, and you are actively considering breaking your vows of fidelity or seeking a divorce.

The seventh box is the "sever, sever box." The marriage is ended; the vows are broken.

> HOPE TO BOX

> SEVER, SEVER BOX

🌟 **Look at the boxes below. Write your initials in the box that best describes your marriage.**

☐	The Never, Never Box
☐	The Hope Not Box
☐	The Probably Not Box
☐	The Maybe Crisis Box
☐	The Probably Will Box
☐	The Hope to Box
☐	The Sever, Sever Box

As you move out of the never, never box on your way to the sever, sever box, the first step in failing to guard your marriage relationship is mental disloyalty. No one but you knows that you have entertained thoughts that were not entirely faithful to your spouse. But the seed has been planted; and as you begin to think even more about another, you become emotionally disloyal. Ultimately you may even become physically disloyal.

Loyalty means staying in the never, never box. It means not even entertaining the thought of being intimate with another person. It means choosing by a volitional act to offer unconditional loyalty to your spouse, no matter what that spouse does. (See Matther 5:27-28 in margin.)

Notice that nothing about guarding your relationship with your spouse suggested that conflict would never occur. Marriages may be made in heaven, but they are lived on earth with human partners. Disagreements will occur. How you handle them will be important, and you may have to renew your promise to yourself to remain in the never, never box in the midst of conflict. Yet conflict itself does not mean you have failed in your marriage relationship.

You can, however, take some practical steps that will help you make your marriage relationship your most important earthly bond.

1. Choose to forsake all competing relationships. When a couple seriously begins to consider getting married, they should choose to

You have heard that it was said to those of old, "You shall not commit adultery." But I say to you that whoever looks at a woman to lust for her has already committed adultery with her in his heart (Matt. 5:27-28).

sever relationships with others they have dated. This should continue after marriage, even when the other person has married. It is easier to guard the relationship by not relating to those to whom you were formerly attracted.

That is good advice for long-term marriages, too. Don't put yourself in compromising positions. If you find yourself at all attracted to a coworker or other acquaintance, maintain a distance that will not invite a deepening relationship. Don't allow situations for one-on-one relationships that could be the first step in getting out of the never, never box.

2. Choose to reorder all priorities. Your biggest competition in a marriage may not be another person. Your relationship with your spouse may be threatened because you place other priorities ahead of your spouse—work, recreation, television, hobbies, sports, etc. Are your priorities in order? What are you willing to sacrifice to guard your marital relationship?

And be kind to one another, tenderhearted, forgiving one another, even as God in Christ forgave you (Eph. 4:32).

Grace: an act of kindness, courtesy, and clemency

Mercy: compassion or forbearance shown especially to an offender

Then Peter came to Him and said, "Lord, how often shall my brother sin against me, and I forgive him? Up to seven times?" Jesus said to him, "I do not say to you, up to seven times, but up to seventy times seven" (Matt. 18:21-22).

☀ **Examine the chart below. In the first column list your personal priorities. In the second column list your spouse's priorities. In the third column list priorities you share.**

My Priorities	Spouse's Priorities	Shared Priorities
_____	_____	_____
_____	_____	_____
_____	_____	_____
_____	_____	_____
_____	_____	_____

Now check with your spouse to see how accurate you were. Which of your priorities takes the most time away from your spouse? Would you give it up or change it in some way to spend more time guarding your relationship with your spouse?

3. Choose to show mercy when your spouse has irritating habits. We all have them, and most of the time we are totally unaware of them. It's OK, even good, to ask your spouse to change. She may hate it when he leaves up the toilet seat. He may hate it when she squeezes the toothpaste in the middle of the tube. But once you've asked the other person to change, show mercy. Make it a joke, not a point of tension. And if your spouse absolutely can't remember, extend your mercy and ignore it. Think of all the qualities you do love, and learn to live with the little habits you might like to change. Remember, some of your irritating habits may be ignored, too!

4. Choose to show grace when your marriage faces real obstacles. Stress, illness, crisis, frustration—circumstances that seem beyond the control of either spouse can add anxiety that mounts and threatens a marriage. He loses his job; she has a prolonged illness; the children are in serious trouble; disagreements occur about caring for older parents. Show grace to your spouse. Pray for God's grace to cling to one another to overcome the obstacle rather than let it divide you. (See Ephesians 4:32.)

5. Choose to forgive when your spouse hurts you. All of us hurt someone we love. It's bound to happen in a marriage. Time and circumstances can make us insensitive or inconsiderate. Sometimes the pressures of a job, the frantic schedules of the children, or exceptional demands around the house just make us forgetful. Nevertheless, the pain occurs. Forgiveness is a choice. Forgiveness means releasing your spouse from punishment for a misdeed. Forgiveness means not bringing up the hurt in later situations. Forgiveness is easier when the other person apologizes and tries to right the wrong. But whether an apology or a reprimand comes from your spouse, the biblical admonition is forgiveness. (See Matthew 18:21-22.)

A Deeper Look

* As we close this discussion on guarding your marital relationship by remaining loyal to your spouse, read Malachi 2:13-14,16 in the margin. Why didn't God receive the people's sacrifices and other acts of worship?

_____

_____

* What are some acts of treachery in a marriage? How can you prevent them?

_____

_____

Pray that God will help you always remain loyal and never act treacherously in your marriage.

Treachery: violation of loyalty or of faith and confidence

And this is the second thing you do:
You cover the altar of the Lord with tears,
With weeping and cryingl
So He does not regard the offering anymore,
Nor receive it with goodwill from your hands.
Yet you say, "For what reason?"
Because the Lord has been witness
Between you and the wife of your youth,
With whom you have dealt treacherously;
Yet she is your companion And your wife by covenant ...
"For the Lord God of Israel says
That He hates divorce,
For it covers one's garment with violence,"
Says the Lord of hosts.
"Therefore take heed to your spirit,
That you do not deal treacherously"
(Malachi 2:13-14,16).

InterACTion

Have you experienced a breakthrough in your marriage? Have you made the personal decision to remain in the never, never box—no matter what? One of the greatest gifts you can give your spouse is to make that decision and then share it. Tell your spouse about your lifelong commitment. Tell your children they never have to worry that you will leave them. Tell your parents and your spouse's parents. Tell your Lord that you have chosen to obey Him. And tell yourself often that this is a promise you intend to keep!

Day 2: Husbands—Fulfill Your Marital Role

Most married couples eventually divide the various responsibilities of living together, but in the beginning of a marriage, they have to figure that out. Generally we come to marriage with certain expectations about who will do what. Looking back to the model of our parents, we may have assumed that the father always took out the trash, washed the car, and did the yard work. And we may have expected the wife to keep house, do the laundry, and provide primary care for the children. More than likely in one spouse's family, the mom did a chore that in the other spouse's family was performed by the dad. Did you encounter those kinds of situations when you first married?

One couple I know faced all sorts of issues like that. When they first married, she discovered that her husband had difficulty discerning some colors. She was inside baking a cake. He was outside painting a door that was supposed to be two different colors. He couldn't tell the difference and was really making a mess. They decided to swap. She painted the door; he finished the cake. Both turned out just fine!

A week later the grass was tall and needed to be cut. He was too busy; she was not. She really enjoyed cutting the grass, but in her family that had been her dad's job. With some embarrassment, she kept wondering what the neighbors must think.

Maybe those days are long forgotten at your house; perhaps you have yet to face those situations. Regardless of the tasks we take on around the house, the Bible has something to say about roles in a marriage. Today we will focus on the husband's role; tomorrow the wife's role. (See Ephesians 5:23.)

For the husband is head of the wife, as also Christ is head of the church; and He is the Savior of the body (Eph. 5:23).

Head: the one in charge, the leader

Ephesians 5 says that the husband is to be the head of the wife. This may or may not have been the situation in the home where you witnessed a mother and father relating. What you saw growing up may influence part of your thinking about the husband's leadership role. The following points emphasize four basic areas or groups of people that influence and define marital roles both positively and negatively.

Culture definitely has an impact on marital roles. Unfortunately the television images of married couples today, both in commercials and the shows themselves, tend to show husbands as weak, selfish, and sexually immoral. Even the macho guys need a woman to tell them what to do. Christians—both men and women—should not approve of this image. It does not value men or women and certainly teaches a poor model to viewers.

Christians provide another view of marital roles. When asked about the married couple you most admired, if you didn't name relatives, you likely named someone in your church. Living models are believable. If they are relating in a certain way and they are happy, then their model may be a good one from which to learn.

Capabilities also tend to define roles. This seems to be a natural extension of the division of chores, like those discussed at the beginning of this chapter. Both men and women can have leadership abilities. Is this the best way to choose a family leader?

Commandments, the clear Word of the Bible, offer the best perspective on the division of roles in a family. As the Ephesians passage says— the husband is the head, the leader, of the family.

✳ **Check the box indicating the influence that has most shaped the leadership model for your family.**

☐ **Culture**   ☐ **Christians**   ☐ **Capabilities**   ☐ **Commandments**

And the Lord God said, "It is not good that man should be alone; I will make him a helper comparable to him" Out of the ground the Lord God formed every beast of the field and every bird of the air, and brought them to Adam to see what he would call them. And whatever Adam called each living creature, that was its name. So Adam gave names to all cattle, to the birds of the air, and to every beast of the field. But for Adam there was not found a helper comparable to him. And the Lord God caused a deep sleep to fall on Adam, and he slept; and He took one of his ribs, and closed up the flesh in its place. Then the rib which the Lord God had taken from man He made into a woman, and He brought her to the man (Gen. 2:18-22).

Ephesians is not the only word from the Lord regarding the roles of husband and wife in marriage. Look at 1 Corinthians 11:8-9: "For man is not *from* woman, but woman *from* man. Nor was man created *for* the woman, but woman *for* the man" (emphasis added).

Two prepositions guide us in understanding these verses. In the first statement, *from* provides a direct relationship between this verse and the creation account in Genesis 2:21-23. Adam was created first, and Eve was created from Adam.

The second preposition is *for*. First Corinthians 11:8-9 makes the point through two statements: "Nor was man created *for* the woman, but woman *for* the man" (emphasis added). The meaning is emphasized by the way it is stated. We again see a direct relationship to the creation account in Genesis 2:18-22. The account speaks of man's loneliness. The animals had mates, but Adam did not. God said that this was not good, so He created Eve. Read Genesis 2:18-22.

The Bible does not indicate that headship is in any way dependent on either the husband's or the wife's capabilities, conduct, or character. Headship comes from creation and God's Word. The issue of headship occurs at the moment of marriage. Until marriage occurs, both are equal in God's sight as far as who is the head of the other. But at the

He must manage his own family well and see that his children obey him with proper respect. (If anyone does not know how to manage his own family, how can he take care of God's church?) (1 Tim. 3:4-5).

time of marriage, God officially delegates the authority of that marriage to the husband.

In 1 Timothy 3, Paul again refers to the man as head of the household, this time in talking about the characteristics of bishops. The word used in 1 Timothy 3:4 regarding headship is *rule*. The meaning is literally "to stand before," implying "to be over, to give attention to, to care for." A similar idea is found in the story of the good Samaritan: "So he went to him and bandaged his wounds, pouring on oil and wine; and he set him on his own animal, brought him to an inn, and took care of him. On the next day, when he departed, he took out two denarii, gave them to the innkeeper, and said to him, 'Take care of him; and whatever more you spend, when I come again, I will repay you' " (Luke 10:34-35, emphasis added). So, *rule* does not mean male domination or harshness; it means giving attention and caring for those you stand before.

✴ **In the space below, write a definition of *rule* as it applies to a husband's role in the family.**

But if anyone does not provide for his own, and especially for those of his household, he has denied the faith and is worse than an unbeliever (1 Tim. 5:8).

Honor: showing respect and admiration

Paul expands this role further in 1 Timothy 5. Although verse 8 is referring to widows, it expands the specific situation to a general principle about providing for all in your household.

The question of headship, according to the Bible, is not *whether* a man will rule his own household, but *what kind of* leader he will be. The Bible is full of both good and bad role models of leadership. Moses is often studied as a positive model; Rehoboam, whom we looked at earlier, was not a good model. Let's look at one example of leadership in the New Testament. In 1 Peter 5:2-3, we find these words: "Shepherd the flock of God which is among you, serving as overseers, not by compulsion but willingly, not for dishonest gain but eagerly; nor as being lords over those entrusted to you, but being examples to the flock." Peter wanted those in authority to lead by example rather than by personal power.

Peter had spoken specifically to husbands about their role earlier in 1 Peter 3:7: "Husbands, likewise, dwell with them with understanding, giving honor to the wife, as to the weaker vessel, and as being heirs together of the grace of life, that your prayers may not be hindered." A husband is to prize his wife and seek to make her aware of her value to him. Acts of kindness, verbal affirmation, gifts, and quality time are measures of honor a husband can bestow on his wife.

A Deeper Look

People who study business learn about leadership styles in management courses. Leaders can be benevolent, caring for those under their authority. They can be dictatorial, making constant demands. They can be laissez-faire leaders, just letting things go and ignoring the results. They can be equipping leaders, helping those under them reach their highest potential, anticipating their needs, and encouraging them to excel. They can be self-serving leaders, demanding high performance and taking all the credit for the results.

❋ Based on Ephesians 5:22-33, what kind of leader should a husband be? Record your thoughts in the space below.

_____

_____

_____

InterACTion

❋ How would you describe the husband's current role in your marriage? Write it in the space below or draw a simple picture to illustrate his role.

❋ If in your marriage you were to follow the biblical guidelines described in the passages you've read today, what changes would be required? Make notes below and discuss them with your spouse.

_____

_____

_____

Pray alone; then pray with your spouse. Continue to pray for your spouse.

Day 3: Wives—Fulfill Your Marital Role

Task: an assigned piece of work

Role: an expected behavior pattern, usually determined by an individual's status in a particular situation or society

A professional friend of mine collects art of women working. In paintings and sculptures she has women preparing vegetables and fruit and canning them, making pralines, selling flowers, kneading bread, making baskets, playing musical instruments, working in a factory, quilting, gardening, making pots, catching fish, herding sheep, picking berries, baking, sweeping, teaching children, washing clothes, churning butter, and sewing. Women have many tasks, don't they?

Draw a simple picture in the space below of yourself, your wife, or your mother performing a task you or she enjoys.

Who can find a virtuous wife? For her worth is far above rubies (Prov. 31:10).

We sometimes confuse task and role. The Bible mentions a variety of tasks women perform. For example, the woman in Proverbs 31 has many tasks. The Bible also tells us about the roles of husband and wife. Today we will focus on the wife's role.

Society continues to debate the whole subject of roles in marriage. Many people believe there should be no role differentiation at all. Their primary argument against the biblical division of roles is that they—not the Bible—have interpreted one role to be better than the other or that one role is more important than the other. That is, being the head of the family is more important than being the helper. Therefore, they say, that means that one person—the head, the man, the husband—is held in higher esteem than the other or valued more than the other—the helper, the woman, the wife.

Let's look at what the Bible really says. It describes the role of the wife in many of the same passages where the role of the husband is defined. In Genesis 2:18, the woman is first assigned the role of helper: "And the Lord God said, 'It is not good that man should be alone; I will make him a helper comparable to him." Eve was created to be Adam's "helper," but she was also created to be "comparable" to him. Her essence was the same: "Bone of my bones And flesh of my flesh" (v. 23).

The Hebrew word for *comparable* means "opposite" or "counterpart." Eve was not created better or worse than Adam, just different, giving the solution of his loneliness a wonderful, complementary side. Even possibly bringing completeness to his incompleteness.

Genesis 1:27 adds to this image of different but equal: "So God created man in His own image; in the image of God He created him; male and female He created them." Both Adam and Eve were created in the image of God. When God addressed Adam and Eve in verse 28, He gave instructions to both of them equally: "Then God blessed them, and God said to them, 'Be fruitful and multiply; fill the earth and subdue it; have dominion over the fish of the sea, over the birds of the air, and over every living thing that moves on the earth.' " Eve was equal to Adam in importance, but her role within marriage was to be the "helper."

✳ Look again at some of the passages we read yesterday. Verses in 1 Corinthians 11 tell us that woman is "from" the man, that man is the "head" of woman. Woman was created "for" the man. In light of these verses, what is a woman's priority? Many women keep house, care for and nurture children, and work outside the home. According to the Bible, what is a wife's first priority?

☐ occupation   ☐ children   ☐ housework   ☐ hobbies

☐ husband   ☐ recreation   ☐ friends   ☐ parents

God created the woman to help the man. God created man to be the head of the woman. These are roles a husband and wife assume when they marry. The husband is to be the leader. Her role is to help her husband accomplish and become everything God created him to be.

Many times wives assume they know how to help their husbands. Often the help they give is in tasks or jobs they create which may or may not matter to their husbands. Consider the following story.

An executive at a company hires an assistant to help him with his work. When he comes to work the next day, she is shopping to buy new drapes for the office. When he asks her to come in so he can dictate a letter, she says she can't because she has scheduled computer training. When he attempts to delegate projects to her, she says she already has too many of her own.

This example is somewhat extreme, but it may offer an illustration of a husband and wife. The wife is busy with many things, and she probably assumes she is helping her husband in doing them.

✳ **How can a wife know she is being a helper? What can she do? Suggest several ideas in the space below.**

_____

_____

_____

_____

One thing a wife can do is ask her husband. Healthy relationships require good communication. Over time in a marriage, spouses get to know each other better and often can predict what the other wants or needs or will say or do. For example, she may know how to prepare his favorite foods just the way he likes them. He may be able to order at a restaurant the very things she would choose.

But tastes change. One couple had been married 20 years. They went into a restaurant. The waitress came to take their drink orders. The man automatically said, "Two iced teas." The woman said, "I think I'll have coffee today." Such a small thing, but it really shocked the man. She hadn't ordered anything but iced tea in years. They laughed about it, thinking how even in little things you have to keep communicating.

Make it a practice of asking each other's opinion and advice. Check signals to ensure you are still on track with your assumptions about likes and dislikes. Spend time together really talking. Then when the wife asks her husband, "How can I help you?" it is a part of a daily routine not a shocking event.

Continue to think about how a wife helps her husband. While he may really appreciate the things she does and she may think that she is helping him, could someone else do those tasks if necessary? What "help" does a wife offer that no one else can give? Maybe it's encouragement or support or faithfully lifting her husband in prayer each day.

One woman told a story about the time she broke her leg. Suddenly she could not do most of the things she normally did around the house. She felt so useless. The situation seemed to be made worse because the rest of the family pitched in and performed all the chores. The house had never looked better. Meals were prepared; laundry was done.

When her husband went in to check on her one day, he found her in tears. Afraid she was in pain, he quickly ran to her and expressed his concern. No, she felt fine, she said. The problem was that she no longer felt needed.

The husband tenderly explained that her unique role was not doing the chores, though he jokingly added that everyone would gladly return them to her when she was able to do them again. Her unique role was as nurturer, security giver, encourager, cheerleader, comforter, and listener. She offered him a helping role in their relationship that no one else could fulfill.

✳ In your marriage what are some unique ways the wife truly helps the husband. List them in the margin; then stop and thank God for that relationship.

A Deeper Look

Wives have many different jobs but only one role. One of the most complete and positive biblical images of a wife is found in Proverbs 31.

✳ Read Proverbs 31:10-31 in your Bible. In the first column below, list the work this wife does; in the other, list the ways she helps her husband.

Works	Helps
_____	_____
_____	_____
_____	_____
_____	_____
_____	_____
_____	_____
_____	_____

InterACTion

Someone has said that behind every great man is an even greater woman ... and a surprised mother-in-law!

✳ What can a wife do to help her husband reach his potential? List some of your ideas below. Share them with your spouse. Do the two of you agree? Can you add to the list together?

_____

_____

_____

Day 4: Husbands: Fulfill Your Marital Responsibility

Jeff and Amy were engaged to be married. They had grown up together in the church, had hardly dated anyone else, and everyone assumed and hoped that someday they would marry. They had gone in separate directions to college, but now had finished their educations and come back home to marry and raise a family. They made an appointment with their pastor to begin planning the wedding and to meet with him for the premarital counseling he required.

During one of the sessions, the pastor turned to the husband-to-be and said, "Jeff, what is your primary responsibility in this marriage?" Without hesitation, Jeff answered, "My responsibility is to provide for Amy and our children—shelter, food, and other needs." He knew he had the right answer.

But much to Jeff's surprise, the pastor responded, "Well, Jeff, the Bible does instruct you to provide for your family. But that's not your primary responsibility to Amy."

The pastor provided the nearly married couple with a list of Scripture references and sent them away with homework before they met again the following week. Let's see what Jeff and Amy learned together.

Love Continually

The husband's primary responsibility to his wife is to love her. A study of the word *love* in Ephesians 5:25 indicates that this verb is in the present tense. In the Greek language this means an ongoing, continuous action—not now and then, not once and for all, but continually and consistently. Just as God continues to love the world and His church, regardless of how people act, so the husband is to love his wife. This love does not depend on a whim, a mood, a circumstance, or an action. It just goes on and on.

Love Actively

Love is both a noun and a verb. In this passage, love is an active, not passive, verb. Active verbs have objects. The object of the husband's love is his wife. If, then, love is an active verb, what actions will a husband do to demonstrate that love?

When Jeff and Amy discussed the actions of love, Amy laughed and said, "One thing my mom says that Dad does to say 'I love you' is to make coffee in the morning. She's just not a morning person; he is. When they first got married, she got up each morning and sleepily started breakfast. By the time she was awake enough to face the day, he had finished his morning jog, read the paper, and taken a shower! Making the coffee was easy for him, but it was a true act of love for her."

Husbands, love your wives, just as Christ also loved the church and gave Himself for her (Eph. 5:25).

Consistent: marked by harmony, regularity, and steadiness; free from variation or contradiction

Continual: ongoing

✳ **In your marriage, what are some large or small actions the husband does to say "I love you" to the wife? List them below.**

_____

_____

Check with your spouse to see how many items are the same.

Love by Choice

The husband isn't encouraged to love his wife, rather he is commanded to love his wife. The decision of whether to love his wife is not his to make nor is it a decision the husband and wife make together. The decision is a choice of whether to follow God's command; a man's decision to love his wife is a commitment made to God.

How can a husband love his wife? He can choose to act for her benefit at all times. He can act with care, tenderness, and with her well-being as the end goal. Even when she is unlovable, he is to love. The decision/commitment is not to be based on emotions but on the will—a conscious choice to love.

Because the Bible commands all husbands to love their wives, ultimately the husband is either in the will of God or out of the will of God. In fact, the husband's relationship with his wife may be the clearest indicator that he has determined to live under the lordship of Christ. Although he may want to separate his relationship with his wife from his relationship to his Savior, he cannot. If he does not love his wife, he is living in known sin, and his relationship with his Lord will suffer. Until the husband is fully obedient to the Lord in his relationship to his wife, he is never in complete fellowship with the Lord.

The relationship between a husband and a wife is the closest earthly relationship two people can experience. God said the two "become one flesh" (Gen. 2:24).

Love Sacrificially

Jeff and Amy spent the evening with her mom and dad. Over sodas and cookies they talked about love in marriage and the husband's responsibility. The evening was getting late. Amy's mom looked down at the almost empty plate. One cookie remained. Her dad looked at her mom and said, "You take it. I want you to have the last cookie."

Later Jeff and Amy talked about that little demonstration of love. Amy's mom had told her during one of their talks together that she had learned not to say too often that she really wanted something—whether a "thing" or his time or something else—because she knew her husband would do whatever he could to make her happy, even at great personal sacrifice. What a marvelous model! (See Ephesians 5:28-29.)

Love suffers long and is kind; love does not envy; love does not parade itself, is not puffed up; does not behave rudely, does not seek its own, is not provoked, thinks no evil; does not rejoice in iniquity, but rejoices in the truth; bears all things, believes all things, hopes all things, endures all things. Love never fails (1 Cor. 13:4-8).

Love: to cherish

So husbands ought to love their own wives as their own bodies; he who loves his wife loves himself. For no one ever hated his own flesh, but nourishes and cherishes it, just as the Lord does the church (Eph. 5:28-29).

The biblical model for a husband to love his wife is Jesus Christ, the supreme example of sacrificial love. The idea isn't that husbands should love their wives because Christ loved the church but in like manner. Sacrificial love costs the giver something. The cost may be material resources; but it may also be time, energy, or devotion.

Crucial to Christ's example is that when He loved His church, He gave Himself. He didn't give a thing, a book, a gift, a letter, a stack of money, or a trip. Christ gave Himself for His church. Things are important, but they are often meaningless if they don't represent and come along with the husband's giving of self. In fact, in some marriages material gifts represent a substitute for a husband's real love.

Because the model most men know is to provide for their wives, they may think they are showing love when they shower their wives with gifts. Many times all the wives really want is to spend time with their husbands, to talk with them, to be with them. If the wife is truly to be her husband's helper, she must spend time with him to know him. When a husband shares with his wife—his time, thoughts, dreams, and visions—and he cares enough to want to share her joys, sorrows, daily frustrations, and victories, then she truly feels loved.

Love Positively

The Bible's only negative admonition regarding the husband's love for his wife is found in Colossians 3:19: "Husbands, love your wives and do not be bitter toward them."

Did you ever have a bad day and take it out on someone you love? Have you ever responded in a harsh tone because you know you didn't follow through on a commitment? You may have had the best intentions, but the pressures of the day crowded out the love action you intended to do. Realizing your own limitations causes you to lash out at the very person you'd intended to receive your love.

Early one morning
  He: "Sure, I'll mail that letter today from the office."
  She: "Thanks so much."
Later that night
  She: "Did you get a chance to mail that letter?"
  He: "Do you think I have nothing to do all day but your silly
  little errands? I have to work hard to support our lifestyle!"

Oops! Not what he intended at all. He really meant to mail the letter. He had a bad day. Caught in his embarrassment over failing to follow through on such a simple request, he takes out his frustration on the one he loves the most.

Has this ever happened to you? If you are a husband who has recently related to your wife with bitterness or harshness, apologize and tell her you really do love her. If you are a wife who has received bitterness, choose to forgive your husband before or whether he ever apologizes.

Love Completely

This session began by looking at love as an act of will, but that does not mean it is void of emotion. Complete love involves all a person is—heart, mind, soul, and strength.

Loving completely also means loving what she loves. Men often tend to focus their attention more on their careers and their own leisure-time activities and the male relationships that result from those interests. Husbands should also willingly give time and attention to her work, friends, and leisure-time activities.

Loving completely means encouraging her to grow spiritually, to reach her potential, to exercise her gifts, and to find fulfillment in serving others. Loving completely means uncovering her needs and providing the love needed so that she can become her best.

Bitter: disagreeable, distressing, severe

Love the Lord your God with all your heart, with all your soul, with all your strength, and with all your mind (Luke 10:27).

A Deeper Look

☀ Based on today's Scripture passages, write a definition of love.

_____

_____

Pray for a fuller understanding of loving as Christ loved.

InterACTion

☀ If you are a husband, show love in action to your wife by doing something special for her. If you are a wife, thank your husband for something he did to demonstrate sacrificial love for you.

Day 5: Wives—Fulfill Your Marital Responsibility

The next week when Jeff and Amy met with their pastor they were better prepared. Jeff quickly told the pastor what he had learned about his primary responsibility to love Amy—continually, sacrificially, unconditionally. But before the pastor could even ask a question, Amy said, "We know that the same passage in Ephesians 5 says that my primary responsibility to Jeff is to be submissive. But when we've tried to talk with our friends about this, they just laugh at us. They tell us that submission is an old-fashioned notion. I must admit that the idea seems a bit foreign to me. I've just spent four years in college, away from home, learning to be independent and make my own decisions. I think I've learned to be a competent, responsible adult.

"But I want to have a biblical marriage, too. I don't want to let a shortcoming in my marriage hurt my relationship with God or with Jeff. I really need some help with this one, Pastor."

The pastor was prepared, too. He said, "Amy, this can be confusing issue for both men and women. It has received so much attention in recent years. In a society that focuses on the rights of the individual, the notion of being 'made' to do something becomes offensive.

"I thought a woman's perspective on this issue might help us all tonight, so I asked my wife to come with me. Last night we were talking about this very subject and about the two of you. She expressed her feelings about this so much better than I ever could. So I asked her to tell you about her experience."

Sarah, the pastor's wife, said, "We got married in a different generation. Fewer women had careers. Husbands, both in churches and in society at-large, were expected to earn an income and make the decisions. No one thought much about it.

"We hadn't been married long when we went to visit some of David's relatives whom I had met only at our wedding. Conversation was friendly but the older couple seemed to be teasing us, trying to provoke a disagreement. I kept deferring to David. So they asked me to answer. I don't remember the topic, but I said, 'David is head of the house. He makes the major decisions.' I can still hear their derisive laughter.

"So I decided to explore my feelings about this whole submission thing. I did it privately, studying my Bible and praying about it. I wanted to make sure I really felt this way and that I was not simply echoing words I had heard all my life in church. This is what I discovered—with the Holy Spirit's help, I believe—deep within myself.

"Although a male 'head of the house' was the norm in those days, I was as independent as anyone. I decided before I married that I would make a conscious choice to join my life with David's, and part of that decision meant no longer being independent. I don't think I made a conscious decision at that time, however, to be 'submissive.'

"During my study about submission, I realized that a quality I had inherited honestly and assumed gladly was to become defiant when I thought anyone was trying to make me do anything. That certainly didn't sound very submissive to me. What was I going to do?

"I continued to pray about this matter, and God turned my thinking away from the word *submission* for a time. I began to think about David. I realized that apart from my salvation and my walk with the Lord, he was without question the greatest gift God had ever given me. I truly believed that he loved me the same way and that our love would endure and grow ever deeper.

"Then my mind switched back to the idea of *submission*. I believed God's Word and that my decision to be submissive should be based solely on what He teaches. I also believed David loved me and I loved him. So what was the big deal? I realized that what bothered me was the notion of being made to do something I didn't want to do. Nothing about my relationship with David was anything I didn't want to do.

"At that moment I chose to obey God's Word and be submissive. David had nothing to do with this decision; it was a choice I made. It was between me and God. In fact, David knew nothing about this process until years later. But it gave me peace.

"It was a good choice. Sometimes I almost feel guilty about it. To me, making decisions for a family and assuming responsibility for them can be a heavy burden. David bears it with grace and love. Through the years he has made some really difficult decisions. So almost all the time I have been thankful that David has willingly committed to be the head of the house. I can't honestly say I agreed with all of his decisions, but I do think he tried to base them on our best interests. He's learned to ask my opinion and not assume he knows what I think about a matter. It takes a lot of pressure off me to turn leadership issues over to him.

"Our life together has been so good that we really don't think about this issue of submission until someone plays it up again. I guess submission is a choice you may have to make again and again. But give it a try. I think you'll be happy you did."

Amy really appreciated Sarah's testimony. It gave her a whole new perspective about submission, and she learned even more about the biblical concept. Amy, Jeff, and David studied and discussed the Scriptures together.

Submission is the woman's responsibility to her husband only. The Bible does not say that all wives are to submit to all men. Ephesians 5:22 says that wives are to submit to their *own* husbands.

Submit: to yield to authority

Wives, submit to your own husbands, as to the Lord (Eph. 5:22).

Submit Continually

As the husband is to love continually, the woman is to submit continually, yielding to him. She may choose at one point in time to be submissive, but the act of submitting goes on and on—even when she disagrees, even when she feels defiant and independent.

Submit Voluntarily

Submit, unlike *love*, is a middle verb. A verb in the middle voice means the subject completes the action of the verb. In this case, the wife submits herself first–and then she comes to her husband in a state of submission. If she feels she is "made to do" something, that is not submission. Submission is yielded, not taken. And she becomes passive, no longer active, in fulfilling her primary responsibility.

Submit by Choice

By definition this is the only way submission works. By biblical command, the wife who does not want to allow sin in her life or to damage her relationship with God will choose to submit.

Wives, submit to your husbands as to the Lord (Eph. 5:22).

Submit "as to the Lord"

Just as believers submit to the Lord, wives submit to their husbands. This is the biblical picture of a Christian marriage.

In effect, the wife is submitting both to God and to her husband—not that she should ever confuse the two! But the two concepts are linked. Since the Lord is the one who commands the wife to submit to her husband, when she submits to her husband she is submitting to the Lord. There is a double level of submission involved. But when she is not submitting to her husband, she cannot be submitting to the Lord. Remember that the command to submit is from God, not the husband.

Servant ministry has long been a concept practiced by Christians in the church who try to live together as the body of Christ. The passage in Ephesians 6 that speaks to servant ministry adds to our understanding of the meaning of submission. Look at verses 6 through 8: "Doing the will of God from the heart, with goodwill doing service, as to the Lord, and not to men, knowing that whatever good anyone does, he will receive the same from the Lord."

Submit in Everything

Wives are to submit everything in marriage to their husbands. Submission "in everything" carries with it the meaning "in all circumstances"—even when the husband is not a Christian.

Now as the church submits to Christ, so also wives should submit to their husbands in everything (Eph. 5:24).

> Wives, likewise, be submissive to your own husbands, that even if some do not obey the word, they, without a word, may be won by the conduct of their wives, when they observe your chaste conduct accompanied by fear. Do not let your adornment be merely outward—arranging the hair, wearing gold, or putting on fine apparel—rather let it be the hidden person of the heart, with the incorruptible beauty of a gentle and quiet spirit, which is very precious in the sight of God (1 Pet. 3:1-4).

Contrary to what some suggest, being submissive does not mean becoming invisible. It doesn't even mean that a wife ought not disagree with her husband. Conflict—disagreements—in marriage are inevitable. If, indeed, a wife brings *everything* into submission, that includes her best thinking, intuition, and ideas. And if she is to be her husband's helper, she will want to share her best with him gladly, even graciously. The notion of submission can change the tone of discussions where a husband and wife disagree from contradiction to contribution. Instead of yelling, "Can't you see ...? Don't you understand ...?" she might say, "Have you ever thought about it this way?" Her contributions then strengthen and encourage her husband.

Although it may be obvious, perhaps our discussion should also specify areas that "submitting in everything" does not include. Since a wife's submission is "as to the Lord," it would not include an expectation that she do anything contrary to God's Word. It would not include anything that would make her willfully sin, commit an illegal act such as selling drugs, or threaten anyone's life, including her own. Submitting, ultimately, is not just something a wife does. It is an attitude. It displays her true character, who she really is—not just the person people see on the outside or think they know.

Whoever desires to become great among you, let him be your servant (Matt. 20:26).

A Deeper Look
God's Word says we are to do as Jesus did. Yesterday as we spoke to husbands we observed how Jesus modeled sacrificial love. Today as we speak of wives, we look to Jesus as He modeled a servant's heart.

✳ **Read Matthew 20:20-28. Then read John 13:1-17. Contrast the two concepts of greatest. How is Jesus' willingness to serve similar to submission? Record your thoughts in the space below.**

_____

_____

_____

Whether you are a husband or a wife, pray that you will follow Christ's example and our Lord's command to fulfill your responsibility in your marriage.

InterACTion
Consider this story: When wearing seat belts first became the law, Darla was furious. There was no way she ever intended to wear one. One afternoon her friend insisted that Darla wear her seat belt, which she reluctantly did. She and her friend were involved in an accident and Darla almost lost her life. She would have had she not been wearing a seat belt. Instead, she received the blessing of life because she submitted to the authority of the seat belt law.

✳ **This story is about rebellion against authority. Why do people rebel against God's Word on wives submitting to their husbands? Write your thoughts below and share them with your spouse.**

_____

_____

_____

Spiritual Breakthroughs I Experienced in My Life This Week

Experiencing Spiritual Breakthroughs in Your Family

VIEWER GUIDE

As you watch the video presentation, fill in the blanks in the statements.

• Most people have more pain and problems in the area of

family than in any other area of life.

• Many parents have _guilt_ about how they raised their children.

• Sitting in the _first chair_ spiritually and maritally doesn't mean you are automatically in the first chair as a parent.

Breakthrough 1: Produce _Godly_ Offspring
(Mal. 2:15)

• God wants both parents to sit in the _first chair_

and then to raise children that sit in the _first chair_.

• Parents who sit in the second chair _hope_ their children

turn turn out _OK_.

• First Chair parents want their children to turn out _godly_.

• Second Chair parents focus on making money and giving their

children a good _education_

Notes: _____

_____

_____

Breakthrough 2: Accept Your _Responsibility_ to Raise _Godly_ Children.
(Ps. 78:4-6; Mal. 4:5-6)

- First Chair parents tell their children about the _works_ of the Lord.

- First Chair parents tell their children about God's _Commandment_

  what is _right_ and what is _wrong_.

- First Chair parents tell their children about God's _Gods work_

  in their _lives_.

- Children today are _Wounded_ by parents who

  Abandon them.

- Children's hurt hearts over time cause them to _back away_ from their parents.

- Children's wounds can develop into _vengeance_ and

  rebellion.

Notes: _____

_____

_____

Breakthrough 3: Forgive Your Own _parent_ and Ask Your Children to _forgive_ You

Notes: _____

_____

_____

WEEKLY STUDY

Train up a child in the way he should go,
And when he is old he will not depart from it (Prov. 22:6).

Key Verse
And these words which I command you today shall be in your heart. You shall teach them diligently to your children, and shall talk of them when you sit in your house, when you walk by the way, when you lie down, and when you rise up (Deut. 6:6-7).

This Week's Study
Day 1: Produce Godly Offspring
Day 2: Teach Your Children God's Works
Day 3: Teach Your Children God's Word
Day 4: Heal the "Parent Wound"
Day 5: Forgive Past Family Hurts

Mike is a young, single adult—one of the most impressive young men around. He has a degree from a major university and holds a prominent position with a telecommunications company. He's popular, attractive, and busy socially.

Mike is also very active in his local church. He attends Sunday School every week. He serves as church treasurer, and he serves on the church's property and space committee. Mike takes his turn caring for preschoolers during the worship service. He's there on Wednesday nights. Occasionally he serves in other ways.

Mike spends one night a month with the homeless as part of the church's Room in the Inn ministry. He tutors children after work once a week at the church's after-school-care program for inner-city youth. Mike does not live in the same state as his parents, so he calls them once a week and tries to go home every month.

Mike had no previous ties with his church when he moved to town; he just came because a family friend recommended it. People began to wonder about this exceptional young man. Those in his Sunday School class know Mike best. Over time this is what they have learned. He has an older brother who is married with children. His father owns his own business; his mother is a schoolteacher. Mike tells stories about the way his father treats his employees, the way his mother works with the cheerleaders, the things his teachers taught him as a child in Sunday School. When Mike talks about why he doesn't drink, he shares a story about his father. When he talks about the biblical example of loving and accepting all kinds of people, he talks about his father's little league team and his mother's students.

Mike obviously was and is loved by his parents and the rest of his family. His parents taught him the works and Word of God. They always made people—first family and then others—a priority.

There is one part of the entire story about Mike that is sad—he's too often an exception. Most churches just aren't filled with young adults like Mike. Why is that? Breakthroughs in this week's sessions will help parents rear more godly children like Mike.

Day 1: Produce Godly Offspring

Beginning in Genesis, God instituted the family as the building block of society. In fact, the Old Testament begins and ends with words about the family. Genesis 2:23-24 says, "And Adam said: 'This is now bone of my bones and flesh of my flesh; she shall be called Woman, because she was taken out of Man.' Therefore a man shall leave his father and mother and be joined to his wife, and they shall become one flesh."

✴ The building blocks below represent the generations in your family from your grandparents through your grandchildren. Write each person's name in the appropriate box (where applicable). Put a *C* in each box where the person is a born-again Christian. Pause to thank God for their Christian witness. Pray that God will strengthen them and you as you seek to pass on your faith to those who have not yet accepted Christ as Savior.

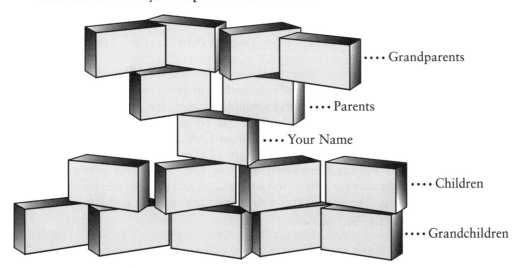

•••• Grandparents

•••• Parents

•••• Your Name

•••• Children

•••• Grandchildren

Near the end of the Old Testament we find an admonition to parents. Where Genesis began with great hope and promise, Malachi carries a warning, a rebuke from God. Malachi 2 addresses unacceptable worship, offerings, and sacrifices. Then we learn why God is displeased. Read Malachi 2:13-15.

What went wrong between Genesis and Malachi? Apparently the people were not honoring God and were disobeying His commandments and by behaving in ways that were not pleasing to God. The message to God's people was essentially, "If you want Me to accept your acts of worship and answer your prayers, you need to get your act together in the way you treat your families." The clear point in this passage is that God intended an enduring relationship between a man and a woman that would produce godly offspring. That's the first family breakthrough—to accept God's directive to produce godly offspring. Your first priority with a family isn't what you produce but whom you produce.

Marriage is not only for companionship and for fulfilling God's creation commands to "become one flesh"; the Lord is seeking something *from* your marriage—something more than you might ever expect. The Lord God is seeking children from your marriage—a certain kind of offspring. God seeks from you godly offspring!

And this is the second thing you do: You cover the altar of the Lord with tears, with weeping and crying; so He does not regard the offering anymore, nor receive it with goodwill from your hands. Yet you say, "For what reason?" Because the Lord has been witness between you and the wife of your youth, with whom you have dealt treacherously; yet she is your companion and your wife by covenant. But did He not make them one, having a remnant of the Spirit? And why one? He seeks godly offspring. Therefore take heed to your spirit, and let none deal treacherously with the wife of his youth (Mal. 2:13-15).

✳ Place an X on the line below to show your level of commitment to raising godly children.

Not Committed   Somewhat Committed   Very Committed

✳ In which chair would your children say you sit? Check one box.

☐ first chair   ☐ second chair   ☐ third chair

Unlike the one time in the universe when God created two human beings in the garden of Eden, other offspring were to come through the covenant marriage relationships of men and women. What God is seeking is not just children, but children who have been raised to choose the way of the Lord Jesus Christ. The Lord wants you to have full integrity and to walk worthy of your calling. Then you are to bring your boys and girls along with you. They are to walk in your footsteps, embrace your values, serve your God, and choose your Lord to be their Lord. The Lord wants you to pass the torch of godliness to the next generation.

✳ If you are married, was one of your main purposes to have godly children? ☐ Yes ☐ No How does your purpose in having children affect the way you relate to your children? Record your thoughts in the space below.

_____

_____

_____

_____

Your priority in raising children isn't only their competence but also their character.

The first-chair person raises godly children; the second-chair person raises children. This isn't by accident or chance. Godly children are developed through intense purpose, perseverance, and prayer; through temporary failures and setbacks; through the ups and downs in life. Beneath it all, deep in the heart of the first-chair person, is the resolve to fulfill God's deep dream—to offer back to Him godly offspring.

Let's look at the story of Hannah and Elkanah. Elkanah had two wives, Hannah and Peninnah. Peninnah had children; Hannah did not. But Hannah wanted children. Every year when she went to Shiloh to worship the Lord, she fasted and prayed and asked God to bless her with children. She promised God that if she could have a son she would make sure he was a godly child, serving God all his life. God heard her prayer, and He gave her a son. Hannah named him Samuel. And when he was old enough to leave home, though still a young boy, she took him back to Shiloh where Hannah thanked God for His goodness and left Samuel to grow up with the priests, praising and serving God. Read 1 Samuel 2:1.

From Hannah's story we learn that:
- Children are a blessing, a gift from God.
- Parents are to thank God for their children.
- Parents are to raise their children to be godly.
- Parents are to offer their children back to God in service to Him.

Thank God for your children. Pray for His help in being a godly parent. Hannah's love was sacrificial. After wanting a child for so long, she gave him back to God as soon as he was old enough to live with Eli.

And Hannah prayed and said: "My heart rejoices in the Lord" (1 Sam. 2:1).

☀ **Have you given your children to God? Do you pray that God will use your children in His service? Or do you desire a different kind of lifestyle for them? Record your hopes for your children.**

_____

_____

Many of society's trends have hurt the family. Less and less children reach adulthood having grown up in a family with both their birth parents still married to one another. Many children today grow up in homes with one parent or perhaps in a blended family. The two-parent biological, family model is no longer as highly valued by our society as in previous generations.

One changing societal trend has been positive, however. The trend is for men to take more responsibility in nurturing their children. This is good. This is biblical! It's the way God intended all along. In 1 Timothy 3:1-7, Paul listed characteristics of elders. These same characteristics include a description of first-chair fathers.
- He rules his own house well.
- His children are submissive to him "with all reverence."
- He validates that he is qualified to lead the church of God by how effectively he leads his own household.

First-chair fathers raise their children with unconditional love and care. First-chair fathers disciple their children and model for them the importance of submission to authority. First-chair fathers earn the genuine respect of their children so that their children submit to them with a heartfelt attitude of reverence.

✳ What was your relationship with your father? In what ways did he move you toward godliness? In what ways do you nurture your children and seek to produce godly children? Record your thoughts below.

_____

_____

A Deeper Look
In week 1, when we considered the faith of Abraham, Isaac, and Jacob, we speculated about Jacob's possible change of direction when he journeyed to meet Esau again.

✳ Read Genesis 33. How did Jacob treat his children in this story? What evidence is there that Jacob cared for his children? that he had their best interests at heart? that he taught them to respect authority? Record your response below.

_____

_____

_____

_____

InterACTion
If you do not have children, talk with your spouse about how you will help pass on the faith to a new generation. If you have children, tell them they are gifts from God and you love them. Tell them your greatest desire for them is that they grow up to love the Lord as you do. Pray for Christian parents and other adults that they will make producing godly children a priority in their lives.

Day 2: Teach Your Children God's Works

Let me tell you about a grandmother I know. Lee is a first-chair Christian, but she did not grow up in a Christian home. When she was young, she and her husband knew they loved each other but felt something was missing in their life together. They turned to God, and He turned their love into a dynamic relationship.

Lee has made it her goal, her purpose in life, to develop godly children. But she didn't stop there. Now every time she gets a chance, she is busy teaching her grandchildren. Lee tells Bible stories at bedtime, and she teaches Bible truths throughout the day. (See 3 John 4.)

Lee has done a good job. All of her children, their spouses, and their children are Christians. The only one who has not yet professed Jesus Christ as Savior and Lord is still in kindergarten, and Lee isn't finished with her yet! Three of her children and grandchildren have gone to seminary and work on church staffs. The older grandchildren and all the children call Lee to share victories and answered prayer.

One of Lee's grandchildren served as a missionary for awhile—the third member of the family to do so. While on the mission field, she called Lee regularly with prayer requests and to report the works of God in her life and ministry. She would be so excited when she talked with Lee that she would breathlessly tell about a miracle God had worked, always ending with, "Now isn't that powerful!"

The works of the Lord are powerful—both those in the Bible and those we experience in our own lives. In fact, the works of the Lord are so powerful that we ought not ever keep them to ourselves. To pass on our faith to future generations, to encourage them to move into the first chair, we must continually share the works of God.

I have no greater joy than to hear that my children walk in truth (3 John 4).

✳ **Is it easier for you to tell your children the stories of God's miraculous works in the Bible or about your own experiences with the Lord? Why? Record your thoughts below.**

_____

_____

_____

A woman told about attending an interdenominational Bible study. She was impressed with the group because there were several hundred people there and all had committed to attend the 16-week course. About midway through the course, the small groups were beginning to feel comfortable together, knowing one another by name, denomination, and walk with God. That night much of the discussion was about the works of God.

Near the end of the session, the leader turned the Bible study toward contemporary application. The leader asked those gathered if they believed people today experience God's works. The woman who told this story began to think of all the ways God had worked in her life, but she waited for others to speak. No one did.

Finally the leader turned to this woman and said, "I guess you think God still works today. Why, I bet God has even done some mighty works in your life."

Teach your children about God's works in the Bible.

Teach your children about God's works in your life.

Not backing off for a moment, the woman replied, "Yes, let me tell you about some times God has encouraged me and times I have personally experienced the mighty works of God." She shared a few of her experiences, then asked others to share theirs.

Several spoke up and said that they were not aware a prayer they had prayed had ever been answered. They seemed surprised to hear people actually expect prayers to be answered and are aware they have been answered. After the session, as the woman drove home to her family, her thoughts turned toward her children. She wondered about the children of those with whom she had shared that evening. What kind of faith would they inherit? Had she, at that time, been aware of the concept of the three chairs, she would have realized that she was sitting in the first chair in her walk with God, and the others in that room were all sitting in the second chair.

※ **How does the spiritual chair you occupy affect your ability to teach and model for your children the works of God.**

_____

_____

_____

_____

For I am not ashamed of the gospel of Christ, for it is the power of God to salvation for everyone who believes (Rom. 1:16).

Psalm 78 instructs fathers to tell their children the works of the Lord. Verse 4 says, "We will not hide them from their children telling to the generation to come the praises of the Lord, and His strength and His wonderful works that He has done." Why would parents fail to tell their children about the works of the Lord? In week 1, a possibility we considered was that parents stopped telling about the ways God worked in previous generations because they had not experienced God in their own lives. This may be the case here. Psalm 78:8 says, "And may not be like their fathers, a stubborn and rebellious generation, a generation that did not set its heart aright, and whose spirit was not faithful to God."

Another possibility might be that the father finds talking about God's mighty works difficult. He may have personally experienced the works of God but questions whether others would believe they were truly works of God. More than that, he may find that he fears becoming emotional when he tells his children about the works of the Lord. Perhaps that kind of emotion would really benefit your children! (See Romans 1:16.)

✳ When was the last time the children in your family saw their father or mother demonstrate deep feelings when they shared how the Lord was working in their lives? Have they seen him become emotional as he shares how God has worked in his own life? Or are they more likely to see him display other emotions? Write a prayer in the space below. Ask God to make you courageous in telling your children about His mighty works.

_____

_____

_____

Return to the key passage for this week, Deuteronomy 6:6-7. This same type admonition to teach God's works and words is found several times in the law of Moses and several times in the Book of Deuteronomy. In this passage, however, the connotation clearly is that teaching children should be ongoing, constant, consistent. Parents were to seize a "teachable moment" but they were also to create them throughout the day.

Have you seen the television advertisements for drug prevention and abuse? A recent one got my attention because it is silent. It shows a father and son sharing a milk shake together. The context is clearly friendly, yet neither speaks for the duration of the commercial. The tag line says, "Another missed opportunity to tell your kids about drugs." As important as that message is, think about how much more important it is to help secure our children's faith by telling them about the works of God.

And you shall teach them the statutes and the laws, and show them the way in which they must walk and the work they must do (Ex. 18:20).

✳ List below opportunities that already exist this week as you drive children to school, as you talk about their day, as you prepare their food, as you tuck them in at night. How many times can you find an opportunity to speak a word for the Lord?

_____

_____

_____

Perhaps one reason the father in the television commercial didn't say anything is because he had nothing to say. You can't teach your children something you don't know. You can't teach them God's works or words if you don't know them yourself. You can't teach them to "love the Lord their God" unless by your example they know that you

Therefore you shall lay up these words of mine in your heart and in your soul, and bind them as a sign on your hand, and they shall be as frontlets between your eyes. You shall teach them to your children, speaking of them when you sit in your house, when you walk by the way, when you lie down, and when you rise up (Deut. 11:18-19).

love God with all your heart. You must first possess the works and words of God before you can pass them on!

Look at Deuteronomy 6:8-9: "You shall bind them as a sign on your hand, and they shall be as frontlets between your eyes. You shall write them on the doorposts of your house and on your gates." In Old Testament Jewish culture, people took that verse literally. They wrote portions of Scripture and placed them in a tiny leather box and strapped them to their forehead and arm. Why? Every time they noticed the box, they thought about God's Word. Even today many Jews have mezuzahs, small parchments of Scripture in a protective container, attached to the side of the main door to their homes. Mezuzahs contain this very passage from Deuteronomy. Every time they come in or go out, they see it and are reminded of their faith and their God. They are also reminded of their responsibility to live faithful lives and speak freely of their God in every context of their everyday lives.

Let us make God's works and words an active part of our lives. Many children and teenagers (and some adults, too) are wearing WWJD? (What would Jesus do?) bracelets, buttons, t-shirts and other apparel. The letters identify them as believers and provide positive peer reinforcement. The letters also remind them to stop and think about what Jesus would do in a given situation.

Such actions let others know your commitment to God in a public way. When you make public your faith, your children realize that's an important part of your life. Which would you rather them think you value more highly, a ball team or their Christian faith? Which kind of label do you show most often?

If you want to leave a legacy, love God. Make your love for Him visible. Talk about the Lord with your children. Take a stand for God in a culture that hates holiness. Sit in the first chair and experience the life-changing power of the Lord in your life, and you will set an example for them to follow.

A Deeper Look

* Turn in your Bible to Exodus. Read chapters 5 through 12 in a contemporary translation or paraphrase. This is a lot to read so you may want to spread it out over a period of time. List on a piece of paper or in a notebook all the works of the Lord in those chapters. Imagine telling your children about experiencing those miracles firsthand. Pray that God will give you the same excitement for telling your children about the miracles in your own life.

InterACTion

Children learn by doing as well as by hearing. Purchase a spiral notebook. Make a list together with your children of the major works of the Lord in the Old Testament and the New Testament. Then list as the works of God in your own extended family. Build your list over a period of time as the works of God in Scripture and in your family come to mind.

Day 3: Teach Your Children God's Word

A youth minister of more than 20 years was telling me about all the changes he had seen over the years. When he began in youth ministry, teenagers were singing musicals and going on retreats. About the worst crisis he ever encountered then was counseling an unwed teenager who was expecting a baby.

That was, of course, a serious crisis and continues to be. But that was a once-a-year crisis in his ministry, and now he may face a crisis that serious almost on a weekly basis. His unconditional love for teenagers and his Christlike approach to calling a sin a sin yet loving the sinner has led students to open up to him. Consequently, he has become involved in the lives of many teenagers. Today he regularly deals with runaways; physical, mental, and sexual abuse victims; violence, including guns and knives being brought to youth events; streetwise kids who have lots of experience with drugs, alcohol, and sex; and homosexuality. He's never become hardened to these lifestyles, but he has come to expect them over the years.

What continues to shock and sadden him, however, is the negative influence of many parents and the lack of awareness of God's Word and standards. Frequently he hears from teenagers who have run away—not because they want to escape the confines of a strict home but because they seek safety from a family that abuses drugs, a parent who parades different partners through the home, or physical abuse from family members or their adult friends.

One story he told illustrates this trend. He had begun the annual True Love Waits promotion challenging teenagers to remain sexually pure until marriage. A young girl who appeared completely innocent came to him privately after the meeting. She said, "After seeing the way my parents have lived, I had already decided on my own that I would never have sex before marriage. In fact, I'm not even sure I'll ever marry. But you seemed tonight to be saying that there's a reason we shouldn't have sex before marriage. Is there some sort of prohibition about that? I thought everybody did it."

He gently told her about God's laws, commandments God told us to obey because He loves us and because they work for our well-being and in the best interests of all humankind. It was the first time she had ever even heard of the Ten Commandments.

A godless generation is growing up in our world today. What steps can we take to ensure that this generation hears about God's Word? This generation sounds much like the one described in Judges 2:10-12.

> When all that generation had been gathered to their fathers, another generation arose after them who did not know the Lord nor the work which He had done for Israel. Then the children of Israel did evil in the sight of the Lord, and served the Baals; and they forsook the Lord God of their fathers, who had brought them out of the land of Egypt; and they followed other gods from among the gods of the people who were all around them, and they bowed down to them; and they provoked the Lord to anger.

How can children be expected to obey God's laws when they've never heard them? How can they hear them without their parents telling them? (See Romans 10:14.) Your children are your priority. Don't depend on their knowing and obeying God's Word simply by hearing what they need to know on Sunday. Besides, how much will they value church teachings if they don't have those truths reinforced during the week?

How then shall they call on Him in whom they have not believed? And how shall they believe in Him of whom they have not heard? (Rom. 10:14).

※ **Remember the dramatic vignette from the video? How much of the Bible do you think the son learned from his father? How has he been influenced by his grandfather?**

_____

_____

_____

Your word I have hidden in my heart, That I might not sin against You (Ps. 119:11).

Today's teenagers are the product of a self-centered generation. Many of their parents rebelled against their parents, against the church, and often against God. Though some have returned to God as adults, many have failed to pass along their faith to the next generation. Many have said, "My parents made me go to church. I'm not going to make my children go. It will just turn them against the church—the way it affected me for many years. Let them decide to go on their own. Besides, they're too busy and too tired to worry about going to church."

✳ Are these parents being obedient to God's command to teach His Word to their children so that each generation will know and obey the Word of God? What advice would you give these parents?

_____

_____

_____

On the other hand, many young adults today have, like grandmother Lee and her husband, discovered a God-sized hole in their lives; but unlike Lee, they have not turned to Christ's church for the answer. In our pluralistic society, the politically correct answer is that all avenues to spirituality are equally good. The only criteria is finding the one that works for you.

✳ What words of advice would you give a person who believes all roads to spirituality are valid?

_____

_____

Nor is there salvation in any other [than Jesus Christ], for there is no other name under heaven given among men by which we must be saved (Acts 4:12).

Again the parents who have not taught their children the Word of God are like the fathers in Psalm 78:8. "A stubborn and rebellious generation, A generation that did not set its heart aright, and whose spirit was not faithful to God."

✳ Which chair do these parents occupy? Explain your answer.

☐ first chair   ☐ second chair   ☐ third chair

_____

_____

_____

✳ What is the best way to teach your child the Word of God? Read the situations on the next page and write your name in the space by the one that best describes your family.

_____ Since our children were infants, they have been a part of our family devotionals. They grew up knowing that their mother and father read the Bible and pray together. We have prayed for them frequently since the day they were born. Now that they are older, they help plan and participate in family devotions. It's our most important time together.

_____ We tried to conduct family devotions. It just never worked. The kids know that their parents always have a devotional together, but the children don't join us. We do encourage them to plan a quiet time of their own, and we make sure they have the resources for that time. But we don't ask any questions about their quiet time.

_____ I read my Bible alone when I can. I usually get up before everyone else. I like my quiet time alone. I have no idea what the rest of the family does.

_____ During some times of the year, such as around Christmas or Easter, we plan special family devotions. We may even light candles and sing hymns. The rest of the year we have separate quiet times, but at least once a week we share what we've been studying in God's Word.

_____ We've tried family devotions from time to time. We've found that not doing them all the time keeps them fresh. The children look forward to the times because they are not routine. We learn Bible stories in other ways, too. We have family contests to memorize a passage of Scripture, the books of the Bible, or something like the Ten Commandments. We play Bible trivia, looking up answers we don't know. We act out Bible stories at bedtime. And in conversations about decisions we must make, we talk about what the Bible says.

_____ I take my children to Sunday School. I expect them to learn about the Bible at church.

If none of these situations describes your way of teaching God's Word to your children, write your own story in the margin.

Do you see any ideas in the situations listed that you'd like to try with your family? Go back and circle them.

A Deeper Look

When Hannah took Samuel to Shiloh, he served the priest Eli. Eli had two sons. Though they were priests themselves, they turned against Eli and against God and were corrupt.

✳ Read about Eli and his sons in 1 Samuel 2:12–3:21; then answer the following questions.

- Was Eli in the ☐ first chair or ☐ second chair?
- Which chair did Eli's sons, Hophni and Phinehas, occupy?
  ☐ first chair ☐ second chair ☐ third chair
- Which chair did Samuel occupy? ☐ first chair ☐ second chair
- Why do you think God punished Eli for the sins of his sons, even though they were grown when they sinned against God?

_____

_____

- Contrast the lives of Eli's sons and Samuel. How do you account for Samuel's godliness and Hophni and Phinehas' ungodliness?

_____

_____

- Do you think Samuel was learning the works and words of God? ☐ Yes ☐ No Why or why not?

_____

_____

Children learn by:
- senses
- reading
- playing
- observing
- questioning
- relating
- discussing
- listening
- doing
- hearing

InterACTion

Children prefer to learn in different ways. Some children are more visual learners. Others learn better by hearing. All children learn by playing and doing. They learn by touching or manipulating figures or through art.

Do you know your own learning style? Your style may or may not be your child's preferred style of learning. But more than likely your tendency will be to select ways of teaching your child in which you are most comfortable learning yourself. Remember that all children learn by doing—not just from seeing or hearing.

You can get an idea about your child's preferred learning style by observing and asking questions: Would you rather watch a video or draw a picture? Would you like me to read you a story, or would you like to act out the story with puppets? We can make a tent like Paul did, or we can sing a song about Jesus. You choose.

✷ Listed below are important biblical areas that parents need to teach their children. Beside each one, list a learning activity that would be appropriate to use with your child(ren).

Teach your children: Learning Activity

• **the Bible is God's book**   _____

• **the two divisions of the Bible**   _____

• **the books of the Bible**   _____

• **the groupings of the Old Testament (law, history, poetry, major prophets, minor prophets)**   _____

• **the groupings of the New Testament (gospels, history, Paul's letters, general letters, prophecy)**   _____

• **stories and verses**   _____

• **how to find special passages**   _____

Day 4: Heal the "Parent Wound"

Sam is like a lot of men today—caught in the middle of caring for aging parents and yet not finished helping his young adult children. He has a stressful job and a lot of uncertainty about his ability to hold on to his position as vice-president in a downsizing business environment.

Sam has unresolved family issues, too. Sam is the oldest of three children, the only son. His sisters think he's their parents' favorite child. He doesn't know if this is so or not, but he does know he has a real wound that his father created. Sam's dad is not too talkative and certainly doesn't verbally express his feelings. Yes, he provided well for his family. He was head of the household. He modeled first-chair faith. He sat in the first chair in his relationship with God, but not as a parent. He never bragged on Sam, never told him he loved him.

When Sam thinks about his childhood and early adult years, he rarely remembers the athletic awards he received. Instead, he remembers the things he did wrong, and there were plenty to remember! Sam knows his father had high expectations for him. He knows his dad was disappointed when he came home with bad grades or a traffic citation. Sam dwells on the fact that he never finished college and wonders if his focus on hard work and achievement in the business world has ever satisfied his father.

When Sam hit the issues of middle age, reflecting on what he had done with his life and whether he had gone the right direction, he began to blame every area of life that disappointed him on his dad. He decided his dad had given bad advice, urging him to stay with a corporation rather than going out on his own. Sam thought about how strict his dad had been when he was a child. Now that his dad was older, Sam was angry when his father didn't always take his advice. Everything about his dad made him angry, and he distanced himself from his parents for the first time in his life.

Sam has never put into words that he failed to receive his father's blessing. He has never admitted, perhaps even to himself, that he longs to hear his father say, "Well done." In the meantime his father wonders what has happened to his son—the son he hunted and fished with, the son who gave him his first grandchild, the son who is just like his father in many, many ways. Has either man voiced the obvious question to each other: What is wrong with this relationship? No!

Sam's immediate family life seems to be going a bit better, but is it? His two girls are grown, one married and one not married. They see him as a good provider and one who likes to give them advice. He has their best interests at heart, but Sam doesn't try to understand before offering advice. He has never bragged on them or said, "I love you."

☀ **Sam has followed in his father's footsteps. He's a good provider and cares about his family. But he also perpetuates the pain that plagues his life. Is Sam a ☐ first-chair or ☐ second-chair Christian parent? Why?**

_____

_____

Unfortunately, by changing a few of the details, Sam's story is a parable for many men and women. Their lives are not whole because they have unresolved issues with their parents, especially their fathers. And the pain they have because of these unresolved issues is an inheritance they are passing on to their children. What can be done to stop this virus that eats away at parent-child relationships?

Birthright: a right, privilege, or possession to which a person is entitled by birth

Blessing: an act or words that invoke divine care, confer prosperity or happiness, endow protection and preservation, bestow favor

Bitter: expressive of severe pain, grief, or regret

For parents to be all they can be, to sit in the first chair of family relationships, they must heal their wounds. They must make relationships with their parents right so that they can have right relationships with their children. Only by dealing with the issues of the past can the relationships of today and the future be healthy and whole.

Although this issue of the "parent wound" seems to be all around us, it is not new. It can surface in any family relationship. Let's return to the story of Isaac and Jacob in Genesis. In Genesis 25, we read about the birth of Esau and Jacob, and we read about Jacob's treachery and persuading Esau to agree to sell him his birthright, as the firstborn son, for a bowl of porridge. In Genesis 27, Jacob again tricked Esau and received Isaac's blessing, the only blessing—the blessing intended for the firstborn son. Instead of looking at Jacob's trickery, however, let's look at Esau's reaction when he discovered that his blessing was gone.

When Esau sold his birthright, he was a young man. He was hungry. His immediate need—hunger—was more important to him than a future inheritance. But when he was older, when not his father's possessions but his formal words of love were to be passed on to him, he wanted that. Esau didn't trade it to Jacob; Jacob took it from him.

Esau went in to Isaac, not knowing that Jacob had received the blessing, and heard this news from his father. "When Esau heard the words of his father, he cried with an exceedingly great and bitter cry, and said to his father, 'Bless me—me also, O my father!'...And Esau said to his father, 'Have you only one blessing, my father? Bless me—me also, O my father!' And Esau lifted up his voice and wept" (Gen. 27:34,38).

Esau was obviously in anguish over what had happened. He had gone out to hunt, to kill game in order to make a savory stew that his father liked and requested. While he was away, his clever brother had once again tricked him out of what was rightfully his. Perhaps Esau's reactions and actions can provide suggestions for Christians today who need to heal the "parent wound."

1. Esau was angry. His anger was justified. Esau had been deceived. Perhaps he was angry at his father. Even though Isaac had nothing to do with Jacob's trickery, Esau may have felt his father had a hand in the plot to keep him away from home until the blessing could be passed on to him. Perhaps, because his father was head of the household, Esau held him responsible. Perhaps he thought his father, even though old and nearly blind, should have been able to tell one son from the other.

Esau was likely angry at his mother. This was not the first time he realized that he was not her favorite child. He probably also felt alienated, distant from his mother. How could he relate to a mother who seemed consistently to put his brother's interests ahead of his own?

He was certainly angry at his brother. Verses 35 and 36 state: " 'Your brother came with deceit and has taken away your blessing.' And Esau said, 'Is he not rightly named Jacob? For he has supplanted me these two times. He took away my birthright, and now look, he has taken away my blessing!' "

More than likely Esau was also angry at himself. After all, he had willingly sold his birthright. He could blame Jacob all he wanted, but at least part of the responsibility in the first act of treachery belonged to Esau; he had been a willing partner. He was angry at himself for not being clever enough to perceive what would take place when he went hunting, perhaps thinking, *I should have known.*

2. Esau blamed his brother. Jacob was, of course, rightly at fault. This is not, however, always the case. We live in a scapegoat society. People rarely want to assume responsibility for their actions. It is easier to find fault with others, to pass the responsibility on to someone else. In families, it is especially easy to blame a sibling for bad relationships with one's parents. This is often the result of jealousy.

Rebekah, Jacob and Esau's mother, clearly showed preferential treatment toward Jacob. Sometimes children are right when they perceive that a sibling is the parent's favorite, but sometimes all the children think the others are held in greater esteem—often without justification.

3. Esau asked if what had been done could be undone. In verse 36, Esau said, "Have you not reserved a blessing for me?" What does this imply? Esau was likely assuming, "Can't you do something about this? After all, you're the head of this household." But it sounds like he either wanted Isaac to reverse the blessing he gave Jacob or he thought Isaac was in on the treachery. If Isaac had truly thought that he had just blessed his firstborn son, Esau, why would he have reserved for him a blessing? Out of the pain we receive from parental hurt, we often cry in agony, wishing the hurt could be eradicated. We wish that life could go on as if the event causing the pain had never happened.

4. Esau wept. When Esau finally realized what had happened and that nothing could be done to reverse it, he wept. This was the beginning of healing for Esau. Although he pledged in anger to kill Jacob (see v. 41), he didn't plan to take this action until his father died. And it was Jacob, not Esau, who ran away from home in fear.

5. Esau asked for a second blessing. Even though Isaac could no longer give Esau the blessing due a firstborn son, he did bless him. Esau received the blessing that should have gone to Jacob.

Even after all that had happened, Esau was still able to ask his father to bless him, and his father did. This is what is needed in so many parent-child relationships. Children need to ask for the blessing if their parents don't initiate it. In many relationships between parents and their adult children, estrangement has resulted as layers of hurt have built up over the years. As the years go by, both parent and child regret the separation but neither is willing to approach the other.

Children often think the parents should take the first step. The children think that since the parents did wrong, they should take the first step to repair the relationship. The parents, meanwhile, are likely thinking that they provided well for their children and the children are just ungrateful. They might admit that they made mistakes, but everyone does. They may think their children should show more respect. Or they may just find it too difficult to say, "I'm sorry."

Esau asked for what he wanted—his father's blessing. That may have taken great courage, and he may not have received all that he wanted, but he did receive Isaac's blessing.

Let's summarize lessons we can apply today to heal these wounds.
- Children can acknowledge their pain.
- Children can identify that pain as coming from a crack, a wedge, or a great divide in their relationship with a parent or parents.
- Children can accept responsibility. If they cannot accept responsibility for their role in causing or receiving the pain, they can accept responsibility for taking action to end the pain by initiating the process of forgiveness.
- Children can be willing, even at great risk, to take steps to restore the relationship. It matters not who takes the first step of forgiveness and reconciliation but that the relationship is restored.

Is your story like Sam's? Is it like Esau's? Briefly list your hurts below. Acknowledge the pain these hurts have caused by circling them.

_____

_____

_____

What actions will you take to heal your "parent wounds?"

_____

_____

A Deeper Look
Blaming others for a predicament did not begin with Esau.

Read Genesis 3:1-13 in your Bible. Whom did Adam blame when God confronted him about eating from the tree from which God had forbidden him to eat? ☐ Eve ☐ God ☐ Eve and God
Whom did Eve blame? ☐ Adam ☐ God ☐ Adam and God

InterACTion

How is your relationship with your parents? Do you need to restore the relationship or make it better? Will confronting the past help? Can you ask for their blessing? Can you say, "I forgive you"? If possible, call your parents today and begin to build a better relationship. If calling is too difficult, write a letter. But make the letter a means of restoring the relationship, not of casting blame.

Day 5: Forgive Past Family Hurts

Brian was called home because his father was dying. Brian was an only child. He'd never had a close relationship with either parent. He spent most of his growing-up years living in boarding schools and summer camps. After high school he went away to the military, then came college, then marriage and life in another state.

Brian may have had a great early childhood—he could hardly remember—but the time and distance between him and his parents had caused their relationship to be formal and distant. Though never unkind to one another, Brian and his parents had little to say when they were together. They came from different worlds.

As a young adult, Brian had been very angry at his parents. He felt abandoned by them. When he met the girl he wanted to marry, his feelings of anger only intensified. Brian saw the close relationship she enjoyed with both of her parents. He appreciated the warmth they offered and the way they invited him into their circle of love, but his resentment against his parents grew and grew.

Over the years, Brian, who had been a second-chair Christian, moved into the first chair. Influenced by his wife and her parents, his faith became more important to him than anything else. His second priority was people—first his wife, then his children, then both extended families, and then others.

Gradually Brian came to realize that the pain his parents had caused him was unintentional. They had grown up in a rural environment and a sheltered world, rarely traveling in their childhood and youth more than a few miles from home. They wanted their only son to have all the advantages they did not have—the best education, summer camps, everything they could afford.

Brian also knew that he had disappointed his parents in many ways. Their values were different from his own, and he had no intention of changing. The values that led them to provide things for him rather than to focus on a relationship with him were consistent with their aim to achieve social standing, position, and wealth.

Although Brian had done well for himself and his family materially and financially, that had never been his highest goal or value. Brian's parents had wanted him to marry a woman of a high class, one whose family held a position in society. He'd married a girl who loved him and who wanted a lifelong relationship with him.

Brian's parents lived in the most prominent house in town; he and his wife chose a home near their church and made it comfortable and inviting for teenagers—their own and others. Brian grew up in a home with parents who wanted to impress; Brian married into a family that wanted to love and serve others. Brian adopted the first-chair values and lifestyle of his wife's family and found joy and happiness there.

While Brian never had as intimate a relationship with his parents as he would have liked, he had never severed the relationship, had never been disrespectful, and had tried to invite them into the joyous life he was living. It had generally been their choice to stay away from a lifestyle they didn't value or understand.

When Brian shared with a coworker that he was going home because his father was critically ill and dying, his friend, whose father had recently died, said, "If your father is still able to communicate, you should confront him. If your father has caused you the pain my father caused me, you shouldn't let him off the hook. You should confront him and tell him what he has done to you. Make him deal with your hurts before he dies."

Forgiveness: giving up resentment of or claim for vengeance for an insult, hurt, or injury

Brian looked at his friend and said, "Why should I do that? Yes, my parents caused me pain. And it took me years to get past that pain. But with God's help, I have long since forgiven them. It was a choice I made. It has enabled me to continue to relate to my parents and to accept that they love me in their own way and tried to do what they thought was best for me. I no longer have any reason to confront my father. God has taken away the pain."

✳ Forgiveness is a lot like some of the other words we've been studying—words like submission. Before you read further, what is the similarity between forgiveness and submission?

_____

_____

_____

_____

Both submission and forgiveness are acts of will. They are not based on emotion, and they are not necessarily earned or deserved by the other party. They are the choice of the one doing the forgiving or the submitting, and they are both God's will in every believer's life. As wives submit to husbands, all Christians submit to God's authority. And God has instructed all Christians to forgive. Jesus frequently taught about forgiving one another. Let's look at some examples. (See John 1:17.)

Jesus was often confronted with Old Testament law. He repeatedly said that He did not come to destroy the law but to fulfill it (Matt. 5:17). As Jesus attempted to move believers from a mind-set of law to one of grace, one of His teachings focused on forgiveness, of not doing just what the law required but going beyond it, not giving people what they deserved but something far better. In Matthew 5:38-42, Jesus said:

> "You have heard that it was said, 'An eye for an eye and a tooth for a tooth.' But I tell you not to resist an evil person. But whoever slaps you on your right cheek, turn the other to him also. If anyone wants to sue you and take away your tunic, let him have your cloak also. And whoever compels you to go one mile, go with him two. Give to him who asks you, and from him who wants to borrow from you do not turn away."

For the law was given through Moses, but grace and truth came through Jesus Christ (John 1:17).

❋ **Is your model for relating to those who have done evil toward you an Old Testament or a New Testament model? If you seek retribution, "an eye for an eye," ask God to help you move to a model of grace.**

Building on Jesus' teaching, Paul taught that we should not harbor revenge when evil has been done to us.

> Repay no one evil for evil. Have regard for good things in the sight of all men. If it is possible, as much as depends on you, live peaceably with all men. Beloved, do not avenge yourselves, but rather give place to wrath; for it is written, "Vengeance is Mine, I will repay," says the Lord.
>
> Therefore "If your enemy hungers, feed him; if he thirsts, give him a drink; for in so doing you will heap coals of fire on his head. Do not be overcome by evil, but overcome evil with good" (Rom. 12:17-21).

Grace and peace be multiplied to you in the knowledge of God and of Jesus our Lord (2 Pet. 1:2).

If we should treat our enemies with such kindness, shouldn't we also be able to treat our family members that way as well?

In addition to leaving with God the responsibility to make things right, to take care of vengeance, Jesus told Peter to forgive and to keep on forgiving—not once, or twice, but seventy times seven. That's 490 times—more times than one person would likely need forgiveness, more times than the forgiver could count.

Forgiveness was such an important issue for Jesus that He included it in His Model Prayer. And He made it conditional: "And forgive us our debts, As we forgive our debtors" (Matt. 6:12). To grant us forgiveness, God expects us to forgive others—even before asking Him to forgive our sins.

Jesus never taught His disciples to do anything He didn't model. Even as Jesus was dying, He chose to forgive those who crucified Him. This took a supreme act of will. Not only did He think it, but with great effort and in excruciating pain, Jesus voiced it for all to hear: "Father, forgive them, for they do not know what they do" (Luke 23:34). Jesus prayed in His dying moments that God would forgive those who had caused such pain. If Jesus could willingly forgive those who crucified Him, we can forgive those who have performed lesser offenses.

✳ **Do you need to forgive your parents for pain they have caused in your life? List the hurts below. Then one by one pray to God, forgiving your parents for each wrong. Then ask God to cleanse you of all bitterness and to forgive you of your sins now that you have forgiven your parents.**

_____

_____

_____

In addition to forgiving our parents, we ought also be willing and able to ask for forgiveness. In the early 1970s the movie *Love Story* made popular the phrase, "Love means never having to say you're sorry." What could be further from the truth? The more we love someone, the greater the likelihood that we will both hurt and be hurt by that person. Saying "I'm sorry" the first time is difficult. It gets easier with practice.

✳ **You may need to say, "I'm sorry" to your children. Answer the following questions to help you decide.**

- **Do you need to say "I'm sorry" because the wounds inflicted by your parents have kept you from giving your children unconditional love?** ☐ Yes ☐ No
- **Do you need to say "I'm sorry" because you thought you knew what they needed but you were really providing them what you needed for yourself and therefore wanted for them?** ☐ Yes ☐ No

- Do you need to say "I'm sorry" because you have been more focused on providing things for them than on passing on your faith? ☐ Yes ☐ No
- Do you need to say "I'm sorry" because you have valued gifts for them more than a relationship with them? ☐ Yes ☐ No
- Do you need to say "I'm sorry" because you have not modeled the best relationship with your spouse? ☐ Yes ☐ No
- Do you need to say "I'm sorry" because your priorities have been reversed and you have been so busy with your job that time for them has been consumed with lesser things?
  ☐ Yes ☐ No

Are there other reasons you should say "I'm sorry" to your children? If so, list them below.

_____

_____

_____

_____

Saying "I'm sorry" is a big step. And it should be something all of us are willing to do. The point of _Love Story_ was not simply that we shouldn't have to say we're sorry, but that love is forgiving—even without apology. That's biblical.

❋ Let's look again at the Bible's love chapter, 1 Corinthians 13. List below all the actions and attributes of love given in 1 Corinthians 13.

_____

_____

_____

_____

Have you extended love like that to your parents? to your children? to your spouse? Ask God to help you love in the ways He has said we should love.

The Bible is specific about loving our children. Ephesians 6:4 and Colossians 3:21 admonish fathers not to anger their children or provoke them, lest they be discouraged. In what ways do fathers today anger or provoke their children?

_____

_____

_____

Discouragement is part of the cycle between parents and children that can eventually lead to total loss of communication and relationships. What steps can Christian parents take to encourage rather than discourage them?

_____

_____

And you, fathers, do not provoke your children to wrath, but bring them up in the training and admonition of the Lord (Eph. 6:4).

Fathers, do not provoke your children, lest they become discouraged (Col. 3:21).

No one can prevent hurts from happening. If nothing else, hurts will come from misunderstandings.

One woman tells the story of growing up as an only child. Every night her mother, whom she saw as distant and caring for things more than her own child, came into her bedroom and laid out the clothes she should wear the next day. As a little girl, she always felt that her mother cared more about her appearance than who she was on the inside. As an adult, she confronted her mother who immediately broke down in tears and told her daughter this story: As a young girl herself, the mother had lived in poverty. Her mother was an alcoholic and never tended to the family's needs. She had gone to bed every night worried because she had no clean clothes to wear the next day and filled with shame that she would have to go to school again in old, dirty clothes. She had wanted to make sure her own daughter never had to worry about such matters. Laying out her daughter's clothes every night had been an intentional act of love that had been misunderstood.

Besides the lack of communication that allowed the hurt to grow between this mother and daughter, the mother could have benefited by understanding that she could have shown love in different ways. Both children and adults tend to give and receive love in certain "languages." Gary Chapman, in *The Five Love Languages,* says that the languages of love include giving gifts, touching, performing acts of service, speaking words of affirmation, and spending quality time with the one you love.

✳ Of the five love languages, which do you prefer to receive? Draw a heart around that love language in the first column. In column 2, rank them from 1 to 5 with 1 being the way you most like to receive love and 5 being the least. In column 3, rank from 1 to 5 the ways you most often show love. Is the order of showing love the same as the order you prefer to receive it?

Love Language	Receive love	Show love
gifts	_____	_____
touch	_____	_____
service	_____	_____
words	_____	_____
time	_____	_____

Your children may not give or receive love in the same language you do. You can determine their preferences by offering them choices and observing their reactions and behaviors. Would you like to go on a picnic or go pick out a new book together? Can I help you with your homework or make you some hot chocolate while you study? Showing love in different languages is one way to enhance communication and understanding and to diminish the number of unintentional hurts.

A Deeper Look

✳ In Matthew 18, Peter asked Jesus how many times he should forgive his brother. He answered with a parable. Read verses 22 through 35. Write a brief interpretation of this story.

_____

_____

_____

InterACTion

✳ Write a letter to each of your children—whatever age, even if your child is an adult (perhaps especially if your child is an adult)—telling each one how much you love him or her. If you need to apologize, do so. Make the letter a treasure they will want to keep.

Spiritual Breakthroughs I Experienced in My Life This Week

_____
_____
_____
_____
_____
_____
_____
_____
_____
_____
_____
_____
_____

CHAPTER 4

Experiencing Spiritual Breakthroughs with God

VIEWER GUIDE

As you watch the video presentation, fill in the blanks in the statements.

- You cannot have a _breakthrough_ with God unless you

  go through _Jesus_ .

Breakthrough 1: Serve God Above Yourself

(Judg. 1:21, 27-31, 33; Col. 3:5) *Coveteousness is idolitry*

Serve the Lord with all your _heart_ .

- The Second Chair has a heart of _Coveteousness_ .

- The Second Chair is filled with _self_ .

- The First Chair gladly _____ to God.

Notes: _____

_____

_____

Breakthrough 2: Sanctify Yourself to God in Holiness

(Josh. 24:23; 2 Tim. 2:19, 21)

_____ yourself of all know _____ .

- _Ask_ the Lord to reveal your sins to you.
- _List_ the sins God reveals to you.
- _prioritize_ your list of sins.
- _Commit_ your list in the next three days.
- _____ to be accountable to one another.

Breakthrough 3: Seek the Lord Yourself
(Rev. 3:19-20)

- The First Chair has a meaningful _relationship_.
- The Second Chair has a sense of _responsibility_.
- The Second Chair must _repent_ to have a meaningful relationship.
- The First Chair must always _seek_ the Lord with all your heart.

Seek the Lord by:

1. Meeting Him _early_.
2. Staying in the Word _regularly_.
3. Praying to the Lord _Continuously_

Notes: _____

_____

_____

WEEKLY STUDY

Key Verse
But seek first the kingdom of God and His righteousness, and all these things shall be added to you (Matt. 6:33).

This Week's Study
Day 1: Choose to Serve the Lord
Day 2: Cleanse the Heart of Covetousness
Day 3: Cleanse Yourself of All Known Sin
Day 4: Pursue a Close Relationship with Christ Through Daily Devotions
Day 5: Practice the Holiness Habits of Prayer and Praise

Something I've learned in life is that the basics always rule. Every successful basketball coach I know emphasizes the basics. He begins team preparation with dribbling, passing, shooting stances, and good footwork. Good coaches don't start with fancy backdoor passes or spinning slams; they focus on the basics. And 9 times out of 10, a team that is good at the basics will beat a team of undisciplined players trying to rely on fancy footwork and exceptional plays.

The truth about basics is operative everywhere—from basketball to heart surgery, from public speaking to writing a best-seller. That's why the pros practice the basics all the time, over and over. Correct understanding and application of the basics control the outcome.

If you want to become a first-chair Christian, one who is truly committed to Christ, you need to realize that spiritual maturity isn't some vast, complicated, intricate, mysterious, or indefinable thing. And the committed are not born with unique traits like a greater intelligence, a better physical appearance, or special intuition.

That's what this chapter is all about—perfecting the basics. Christianity is not simply a religion that gives us a label to wear because our parents professed Christ. It is an individual choice to follow a living Savior. That living God wants fellowship with His followers, and that fellowship can only be strengthened by improving the basics in righteous living that God gave us through His Word and Jesus gave us through His example.

Following the basics will help believers in the second chair move to the first chair, if that is their desire. You will discover some areas of your life that may have been blocking that move. If moving to the first chair is your desire, practicing the basics will help you do that. Once you've moved to the first chair, you can't stop practicing the basics. The closer your walk with God, the more important spiritual disciplines become.

Day 1: Choose to Serve the Lord

The first spiritual breakthrough is simply to choose to serve the Lord. How many times have we dealt with the word *choice* in these studies? Submission is a choice. Forgiveness is a choice. Serving God is a choice.

✳ **At the beginning of each new year, do you make resolutions?**
☐ Yes ☐ No
What area of your life is usually the focus of your resolutions?

How determined are you to keep your resolutions?

_____

_____

How long do they last?
☐ 1 day   ☐ 1 week   ☐ 1 month   ☐ all year

Often our annual resolutions are the same year after year, because we don't have the desire or the discipline to follow through with what it takes to reach the goal. Two of the most frequent resolutions for Americans today deal with weight loss and exercise. Both of these goals mean changes in the basics of how we live our lives. The key to weight loss is not some magic formula that will once and for always eradicate the pounds that may have been years in accumulating. Rather the secret to weight loss is eating a healthy, balanced diet while adding nutrient-rich foods and eliminating fat and calorie-laden foods.

Exercise is the same. Buying expensive equipment and fashionable workout attire or joining a health club will not make you fit. Only the discipline of daily exercise will make a difference.

Most resolutions fail within the first few weeks. Why is that? Essentially it is because we have not practiced the lifestyle-changing basics to make them a part of our everyday lives. If we could maintain our resolutions for three months, they would become habits. After that, we would want to continue to do them.

How much more shall the blood of Christ, who through the eternal Spirit offered Himself without spot to God, cleanse your conscience from dead works to serve the living God? (Heb. 9:14).

✺ **Consider an area in your life in which you have excelled—a sport, a musical instrument, a craft. Identify the basics.**

_____

_____

Seek: to go in search of

Serve: to contribute, to provide, to assist; to be worthy of reliance or trust

How long did it take you to master the basics? _____

How did you feel when you reached some level of success?

_____

How do you serve God? *Serve* is one of those active verbs we talked about earlier. Those serving are doing something, not having something done for them. God expects our faith to have action. Let's look at some Scriptures that give us some guidance about serving our Lord.

1. Give up whatever stands between you and God. Fellowship with God means that whatever is keeping a person in the second chair will become unimportant, or God will provide it once a person yields to God and moves into the first chair. Our role is to seek and to serve. Jesus gave this teaching early in His ministry as part of the Sermon on the Mount:

> So why do you worry about clothing? Consider the lilies of the field, how they grow: they neither toil nor spin; and yet I say to you that even Solomon in all his glory was not arrayed like one of these. Now if God so clothes the grass of the field, which today is, and tomorrow is thrown into the oven, will He not much more clothe you, O you of little faith? Therefore do not worry, saying, "What shall we eat?" or "What shall we drink?" or "What shall we wear?" For after all these things the Gentiles seek. For your heavenly Father knows that you need all these things. But seek first the kingdom of God and His righteousness, and all these things shall be added to you (Matt. 6:28-33).

✳ **What needs, worries, or fears keep you from yielding completely to God and moving into the first chair? List them below. Pray concerning each item that God will provide for your need and that you will yield your life totally to Him.**

_____

_____

_____

You shall love the Lord your God with all your heart, with all your soul, and with all your mind. ...You shall love your neighbor as yourself (Matt. 22:37,39).

Inasmuch as you did it to one of the least of these My brethren, you did it to Me (Matt. 25:40).

Thanks be to God for His indescribable gift! (2 Cor. 9:15).

2. Put your faith into action. Paul built on the teachings of Jesus and also encouraged believers to do good works. He wrote to the Ephesians: "For by grace you have been saved through faith, and that not of yourselves; it is the gift of God, not of works, lest anyone should boast. For we are His workmanship, created in Christ Jesus for good works, which God prepared beforehand that we should walk in them" (Eph. 2:8-10). Paul wanted to make certain all believers first understood that salvation is a free gift. For many believers, even today, receiving a gift is difficult. Many would rather be giving than receiving. And to receive so great a gift as salvation, we think surely we must earn it. We cannot earn salvation; but we, because we love and choose to serve the God of our salvation, can do good works.

Christians should be known by the works they do. They should be the first in line to feed the hungry, care for the poor, visit those who are sick and in prisons. That is part of what serving God means.

✴ What opportunities for "good works" does your church provide? In which ones are you active? Make a list of opportunities below and circle the ones in which you are currently involved. Place a checkmark by those that interest you.

By this My Father is glorified, that you bear much fruit; so you will be My disciples (John 15:8).

_____

_____

_____

_____

3. Minister in Jesus' name. When you "do good works," how do the people to whom you minister know you come in Jesus' name? Do you tell them? As much as God expects Christians to care for others and meet their needs, He also expects us to tell others about Him. In John's Gospel we find Jesus saying, "You did not choose Me, but I chose you and appointed you that you should go and bear fruit, and that your fruit should remain, that whatever you ask the Father in My name He may give you. These things I command you, that you love one another" (John 15:16-17). In serving God we are to tell others that the gifts we offer are in His name and the greatest gift is the one we have received—salvation through Christ Jesus.

The Bible also cautions believers not to forget the motivation for their good works and fruit-bearing activities. More than likely you know some people who are very active in church but still sit in the second chair. You may even be one of them! They have replaced the basics of a daily walk with Christ with the routine of coming to His house. But they are so busy with unimportant things that they have forgotten the purpose of attending church—to worship the God of the universe.

Remember the story of Mary and Martha. Jesus was the guest at the home of Mary, Martha, and Lazarus. Martha wanted to provide the best for her honored guest, while Mary wanted to sit at Jesus' feet, not missing a moment of being with Him and hearing what He had to say. The Bible says, "Martha was distracted with much serving" (Luke 10:40). She even went to Jesus to complain about Mary, but Jesus gently reminded her about her priorities: "Martha, Martha, you are worried and troubled about many things. But one thing is needed, and Mary has chosen that good part, which will not be taken away from her" (Luke 10:41-42).

Sometimes when people are "busy doing the Lord's work," they are sincerely seeking God. Sometimes their work began as a service to God and to His people, but eventually the service itself was so satisfying that

Take heed that you do not do your charitable deeds before men, to be seen by them. Otherwise you have no reward from your Father in heaven. Therefore, when you do a charitable deed, do not sound a trumpet before you as the hypocrites do in the synagogues and in the streets, that they may have glory from men. Assuredly, I say to you, they have their reward (Matt. 6:1-4).

it took the place of God in their lives. And sometimes the actions were nothing more than an avenue to receive praise and recognition.

※ **What is your motivation for service? How can you keep your focus on God in your busyness?**

_____

_____

A Deeper Look
Once we've established the basics, we're ready to build on them. We learned earlier that first-chair Christians focus on people. Jesus frequently said that by serving others we serve Him.

※ **Read Matthew 25:31-46 in your Bible. What does Jesus say about serving others? Whom should we serve? Why?**

_____

_____

_____

InterACTion
If you do not know about opportunities for ministry in or through your church, ask someone involved to talk with you about this. If your church is not involved in such ministries, speak with a church leader about starting one, or find community agencies that need your help. Take this step to seek and serve Jesus. Pray for God's guidance in selecting the area of service where He would have you serve.

Day 2: Cleanse the Heart of Covetousness

Many believers sit in the second chair, the chair of compromise. They make other people take a backseat. They do not love, serve, or pray for others on a regular basis. Something else always takes priority, and that "something" soon determines everything in that person's life.

If you are sitting in the first chair as you read this section, you will probably experience moments of affirmation about some of the hard decisions you have made because of your commitment to the Lord. If, on the other hand, you sit in the second chair, you might come face-to-face with some giants that still wander the mountains and valleys of your life. Giants are powerful and painful to deal with, but they can be defeated through commitment. You can find liberty, freedom, fulfillment, and joy, but the journey will not be easy.

If a believer's life is not filled with love for others, service to others, and prayer for others, what fills it? Each of us pursues what we consciously or subconsciously find appealing because life must be full of something. The more appealing something is to us, the more passionate and focused we are about it, and the more we dedicate our thoughts, time, and energy to attaining it.

The person who doesn't choose to pursue and serve the Lord and His people has many other options, but nearly anything else you choose to fill your life fits one of these four categories:

1. Desire to acquire possessions—getting or saving great amounts
2. Desire for personal pleasure—enjoying leisure or sensuality
3. Desire for power and prestige—controlling and being in charge
4. Desire to serve people—serving the needs of others

For each of the four "desires," list one contemporary example.

1. Possessions: _____

2. Personal pleasure: _____

3. Power and prestige: _____

4. Serve people: _____

Rank the four categories in the order of their pull on your life. Which one of the first three most often stands in the way of serving God and others? Put a checkmark by it. Pray right now for God's power to release you from its control.

How does this fit into the principle of the three chairs? How you spend your time and money are evidences of your beliefs. Your behavior reveals the chair in which you sit.

We have often spoken of the desire for material gain for two reasons. First, the Bible frequently speaks of this sin, and biblical examples of people who did not walk closely with God often were guilty of it. Second, this desire is a major obstacle between many Christians and God today. Our society values the accumulation of wealth. If people are wealthy, they are hard working not lazy; they are smart; they are clever; and generally they are seen as attractive. Their lifestyle is something to emulate, aspire to, dream about. Wealthy people are envied.

Look at the evidence of this. A player in any sports league is known for the records he breaks and the money he makes. Movie stars are ranked by the salaries they command and the box office receipts of

Covetousness: inordinate desire for wealth or possessions

Idolatry: the worship of a physical object as a god; immoderate attachment or devotion to something

Contentment: the state or quality of being satisfied with what one has or one's status in life

Let your conduct be without covetousness; be content with such things as you have (Heb. 13:5).

their movies. Television personalities and business entrepreneurs are ranked in business journals by their salaries and their wealth.

The New Testament writers included covetousness in lists of sins. Look at Colossians 3:5: "Therefore put to death your members which are on the earth: fornication, uncleanness, passion, evil desire, and covetousness, which is idolatry." Since material gain is so highly rated in our contemporary culture, it is difficult for us to regard greed as a sin, isn't it?

Things themselves are not the problem. The problem is allowing them to come between you and God. The problem is worrying more about one more dollar than about your walk with God. The problem is holding on to the dollar so tightly that you cannot release even a bit of your wealth to help those in need. The problem is that your wealth tends to make you self-satisfied, as if you did not need God at all and attained all that you have on your own. Our society suggests that money can buy everything worth having, and we believe that lie. The problem is that all people are created with an emptiness only God can fill, and wealth leads us to seek other ways to fill the emptiness.

In one church I attended, a man had gone into business for himself. He began with nothing; but entering the business, he said: "I will do nothing without God. God will be my business partner. In fact, God will be the managing partner." So throughout his career he gave God 51 percent of his earnings. Was it easy? Probably not. It was difficult when he started out and had nothing. Half of a little is a lot when you are struggling to establish a business. Then half his money became a lot of money when he was successful, but he may have been less dependent on it because he was already in the habit of giving.

☀ What percentage of your income do you give to your local church? _____% What percentage of your income do you give each year to institutions beyond your church?_____% When you give to charitable institutions, do you consider that a gift to God? ☐ Yes ☐ No

Let the box below represent 100 percent of your income. Shade the portion you give to God.

0%   100%

While preaching on stewardship, one pastor said that one aspect of giving is simply saying, "I don't need that." In a world where consumers are bombarded with commercials from newspapers, magazines, radio, television, movies, the internet, tons of unsolicited catalogs, and billboards, making the statement that we are content with what we have is a radical Christian stance. In some ways it may be one of the boldest ways we can proclaim our Christianity today.

A Deeper Look

✳ Read 1 Timothy 6:6-10. Why is contentment like godliness? What two physical needs does Paul name? What happens to people who are greedy? What sorrows do rich people have? Record your answers on a separate sheet of paper.

InterACTion
What is the last thing you bought for yourself? How much did it cost? Consider writing a check for the same amount and give it to your church or a charitable organization in your community.

Day 3: Cleanse Yourself of All Known Sin

How would you like a hands-on, practical approach to discovering and, with God's help, eliminating sins from your life? Every time a Christian can remove a sin from his or her life, Satan is defeated and the believer walks in closer harmony with God.

Becoming more like God means finding sins, repenting of them, and restoring relationships with people and with God. It isn't an easy process. In fact, it is often very painful. When Christians open themselves to God and ask Him to help them rid their lives of sin, God will reveal to them sins they never knew they committed. What a humbling experience.

The goal of eliminating sin is to grow in holiness. Look at what Paul said to Timothy concerning sin and holiness: "Let everyone who names the name of Christ depart from iniquity. ... Therefore if anyone cleanses himself ..., he will be a vessel for honor, sanctified and useful for the Master, prepared for every good work (2 Tim. 2:19,21).

✳ In 2 Timothy, Paul suggests a two-step process. What are the steps from sin to holiness?

1. _____

2. _____

Hebrews 12:1-2 also suggests two steps to holiness: "Let us lay aside every weight, and the sin which so easily ensnares us, and let us run with endurance the race that is set before us, looking unto Jesus, the author and finisher of our faith."

Now godliness with contentment is great gain. For we brought nothing into this world, and it is certain we can carry nothing out. And having food and clothing, with these we shall be content. But those who desire to be rich fall into temptation and a snare, and into many foolish and harmful lusts which drown men in destruction and perdition. For the love of money is a root of all kinds of evil, for which some have strayed from the faith in their greediness, and pierced themselves through with many sorrows (1 Timothy 6:6-10).

Sin: an offense against God; a shortcoming, a fault

Holiness: devoted entirely to God

If we say that we have no sin, we deceive ourselves, and the truth is not in us. If we confess our sins, He is faithful and just to forgive us our sins and to cleanse us from all unrighteousness (1 John 1:8-9).

If My people who are called by My name will humble themselves, and pray and seek My face, and turn from their wicked ways, then I will hear from heaven, and will forgive their sin and heal their land (2 Chron. 7:14).

Beloved, let us cleanse ourselves from all filthiness of the flesh and spirit, perfecting holiness in the fear of God (2 Cor. 7:1).

What are the two steps in Hebrews 12?

1. _____

2. _____

How are they alike/different from the passage in 2 Timothy?

_____

_____

How is sin like a weight?

_____

_____

In both passages the author clearly assumes that his readers need to cleanse themselves from present sin and pursue righteousness and Jesus? Don't allow yourself to believe, even for an instant, that you are an exception to these two admonitions! (See John 1:8-9.)

Cleansing yourself from all known sin is one of the most difficult things for a believer to do. If you are an average Christian today, you may not have thought a great deal about your sin. But the threshold to growth in personal holiness is through the cleansing of personal sin.

You may have rationalized or been defensive about certain areas of sin in your life. When you move toward holiness, you want to get sin out of your life. The greater you desire holiness, the more willing you become to pay whatever the price to be fully cleansed, to have a clean conscience before God. (See 2 Chronicles 7:14.)

How do you honestly feel about sin in your life? Look at the list below and circle the statement that best describes you.
1. I actively pursue personal sin.
2. I don't think much about it; sin just happens.
3. I try to avoid sin most of the time.
4. I feel regret when I sin.
5. I become angry when I sin.
6. I become deeply grieved when I sin.
7. I hate and detest sin.

The reasons many believers experience such frustration and defeat in their spiritual lives is due to the accumulation of unconfessed and unprocessed sins lying beneath the surface. Confession is the required component both for forgiveness as well as cleansing of all our unrighteousness. We choose to go to the Lord, and He chooses to cleanse us.

Here is a 10-step process from *Personal Holiness in Times of Temptation* that you can use to experience personal cleansing that will result in freedom and joy.

Restoration: to renew to the condition of the original state

Be of good cheer; your sins are forgiven you (Matt. 9:2).

For I will be merciful to their unrighteousness, and their sins and their lawless deeds I will remember no more (Heb. 8:12).

EXPERIENCE PERSONAL CLEANSING

1. Sit alone in a quiet place for at least an hour with blank paper, a pen, and a Bible.
2. Quiet your heart by sitting still, closing your eyes, and preparing to seek the Lord. Put all distractions and worries out of your mind. Remain at His throne until you know you are quiet before Him. Don't be frustrated; this may take time.
3. Pray to the Lord and thank Him for bringing you to this place in your life where you desire to be cleansed. Ask Him to give you courage and grace as you humble yourself before Him. Commit to the Lord that you will not run away but that you will stay in His presence until He reveals that you are fully cleansed. Prepare your heart and commit to completing the process regardless of the cost or consequences to you.
4. Ask the Holy Spirit to reveal specific sins in your life between you and God.
5. List everything the Holy Spirit reveals to you. Don't hesitate, don't rationalize, and don't give in to the temptation to skip some of the harder ones. When your list is complete, number the sins in the order of how difficult they will be for you to confess and make restoration, with one being the most difficult.
6. Confess your sins one at a time before the Lord. Begin with the most difficult. Then, one by one, go through your list until you are finished.
7. Anticipate the personal desire to flee this process. Give yourself three days to make right every item on your list.
8. Expect to humble yourself to others in the process.
9. After you have confessed and made restoration, burn your list.
10. Thank God for His cleansing. Praise Him for His forgiveness.

Therefore if you bring your gift to the altar, and there remember that your brother has something against you, leave your gift there before the altar, and go your way. First be reconciled to your brother, and then come and offer your gift (Matt. 5:23-24).

Go and sin no more (John 8:11).

A Deeper Look

Read Matthew 5:23-24. What happens when we try to worship God with unconfessed sin against another in our lives? Is prayer, asking God's forgiveness, enough? What does this passage say we should do?

_____

_____

_____

InterACTion

With whom would you like to restore a relationship? Identify that person(s) and take steps to do that today.

Day 4: Pursue a Close Relationship with God Through Daily Devotions

Habit: a behavior pattern acquired by frequent repetition

Holding fast the word of life, so that I may rejoice in the day of Christ that I have not run in vain or labored in vain (Phil. 2:16).

Habits create our character. Your destiny is ultimately controlled by the habits of your life and thoughts.

When a habit is built, character is formed. When you think about it, character is the sum total of a person's habitual traits and qualities. When a major habit changes, that part of the person's character changes. For instance, if a person habitually lies, his character becomes untrustworthy. If he learns to tell the truth, his character becomes fully trustworthy.

If you want a closer walk with God, you may need to change some of your habits. Our journey with Christ begins the moment we accept Him as our personal Savior. At that time, the Lord draws us unto Himself as His child and a member of His family. From that point forward, the Lord calls us to be transformed into the image of Christ. As time goes on, we should be exemplifying the identical traits of Christ's character—love, joy, peace, long-suffering, kindness, goodness, faithfulness, gentleness, and self-control.

One of the main habits Christians should develop is a daily devotional time. Have you tried to establish a daily devotion? What happened? Record your experience below.

_____

_____

What is currently the center of your life? Check one.

- [ ] work/business
- [ ] children
- [ ] leisure activities
- [ ] God
- [ ] marriage
- [ ] church
- [ ] money
- [ ] other: _____

Whatever priority you selected, how long would you be willing to neglect it? _____

How often does God get your full attention? Check one.

- [ ] daily
- [ ] twice a week
- [ ] weekly
- [ ] monthly
- [ ] other: _____

For whoever is ashamed of Me and My words, of him the Son of Man will be ashamed when He comes in His own glory (Luke 9:26).

For the word of God is living and powerful, and sharper than any two-edged sword, piercing even to the division of soul and spirit, and of joints and marrow, and is a discerner of the thoughts and intents of the heart (Heb. 4:12).

But the word of the Lord endures forever (1 Pet. 1:25).

Whatever is at the center of your life must be moved so the Lord and your time with Him reigns as the central focus. The single most strategic change you can make to grow closer to God is to put your daily devotional habit first on your priority list.

The focus of daily devotions isn't the specific procedures one follows but one's intimate relationship with the Lord. Because you are devoted to the Lord, you choose to dedicate priority time each day to Him. And because He is the most important person in the world to you, you do not allow anyone or anything to take precedence over Him.

Here are a few tips from *Personal Holiness in Times of Temptation* to maximize your devotional habit.

1. Select a place. The first key to successful devotions is to identify your favorite location in the house to be alone with God. The place should be comfortable, absolutely quiet, and as private as possible.

2. Schedule a time. Morning is the best time for me to be alone with God. I have tried other times, but morning is best. To establish a habit you may have to alter your routine, get to bed earlier, or live with less sleep.

Whatever you decide, meet the Lord at the same time each day throughout the week. You may decide to change the time a bit on weekends. That will depend on your personal schedule.

3. Structure your agenda. Nothing seems to ruin good intentions faster than having no plan. When you get up in the morning and go to your devotional place, you should know what you are going to do during that time alone with God. That is not the time to decide.

Heaven and earth will pass away, but My words will by no means pass away (Mark 13:31).

Let the word of Christ dwell in you richly in all wisdom, teaching and admonishing one another in psalms and hymns and spiritual songs, singing with grace in your hearts to the Lord (Col. 3:16).

And take the helmet of salvation, and the sword of the Spirit, which is the word of God (Eph. 6:17).

The grass withers, the flower fades,
But the word of our God stands forever (Isa. 40:8).

Take the complexity out of life! Build a routine which you follow each morning. I change my routine once a year. That way, when I get to my devotional corner, I don't waste a moment. Figure out what works for you. You may need a few weeks to decide what you really like and what feels comfortable. Then make the routine part of your habit. By incorporating this into your lifestyle, you don't have to reinvent your devotional process every morning or every week.

Let me also encourage you not to become legalistic in your walk with the Lord. Your devotions should be flexible, allowing for emergencies, exhaustion, and unexpected situations.

On one recent morning, following an exhausting day of counseling late into the night, I arose so emotionally and physically drained that I simply enjoyed the presence of the Lord in quietness. I didn't follow my normal schedule, didn't pray through my prayer list, didn't write in my journal, and didn't even read my Bible. I just sat in the presence of the Lord for an hour.

4. Begin with whatever is most enjoyable to you. Some people read devotional books or biographies of Christian heroes. Some listen to praise recordings. Begin with something encouraging or uplifting. This is your time with the Lord.

5. When you are ready to turn your heart toward the Lord, stop and prepare yourself for Him. Close your eyes and quiet your heart. Bring all your thoughts into sharp focus on God. Do not permit interfering or distracting thoughts to conquer your intention. This will likely be difficult at first. Don't become frustrated. Eventually, bringing your heart into focus will take only a few seconds.

6. Follow your schedule in the same order each day. Avoid the temptation to skip a step. If you find that you are frequently tempted to eliminate a certain step, try to discover the reason. Remain focused on God.

7. Whatever items you include in your daily quiet time, always include prayer and the Word of God. Never let reading a book substitute for reading the Bible. Reading about the Bible is not the same as reading God's Holy Word. Don't shorten the amount of time you pray. At least half the time set aside should be Bible reading and prayer.

8. Realize that you will likely miss some days. Plan in advance what you will do when this happens. Don't try to make up the time. Just pick back up where you left off. Never permit yourself to construct a mountain you must conquer to make yourself "pay" for neglecting the Lord. Christ paid for all your sins and all of mine. His payment was sufficient for the Father, so it must also be for you. Just apologize to the Lord as you would to another friend for neglecting him or her and receive His forgiveness and warm embrace. He missed your fellowship more than you missed His. Remember, no relationship flourishes long if it is based merely on guilt and obligation.

✳ Perhaps you have never thought about elements to include in a daily quiet time with God. Check those that would be meaningful to you.

☐ Bible reading   ☐ journaling

☐ listening to Christian music   ☐ praise

☐ reading a Christian book   ☐ prayer

☐ using a devotional guide

List other elements you'd like to include.

_____

_____

For the word of the Lord is right (Ps. 33:4).

"Is not My word like a fire?" says the Lord, "And like a hammer that breaks the rock in pieces?" (Jer. 23:29).

Of all the elements listed, the one that is the most essential and the one that will transform your life the most, helping you to conform to Christ, is reading the Bible. The Holy Spirit uses God's Word as His primary tool of transformation.

A good plan is to read through the Bible every year. Or follow a devotional guide that will include selected passages from all types of biblical writing.[1]

Choose passages that speak to areas in which you need transformation; then meditate on those verses until you commit them to memory. As God's Word takes root in your heart, change will come in your life.

Pray the Scriptures. Choose passages that are particularly meaningful to you and pray them back to the Lord. Scripture selections which lend themselves to this approach are found in Psalms, Proverbs, Ephesians, Colossians, and Philippians.

Change the way you look at the Bible. The Bible is a priceless gift from the Lord for the entire body of Christ as well as for each member of the body. The more you align your life with the Bible and use it for its intended purposes, the more you will experience the fulfillment of God's promise of your transformation into the very image of Jesus Christ.

The word is near you, in your mouth and in your heart (Rom. 10:8).

"Now the parable is this: The seed is the word of God. Those by the wayside are the ones who hear; then the devil comes and takes away the word out of their hearts, lest they should believe and be saved. But the ones on the rock are those who, when they hear, receive the word with joy; and these have no root, who believe for a while and in time of temptation fall away. Now the ones that fell among the thorns are those who, when they have heard, go out and are choked with cares, riches, and pleasures of life, and bring no fruit to maturity. But the ones that fell on the good ground are those who, having heard the word with a noble and good heart, keep it and bear fruit with patience (Luke 8: 11-15).

A Deeper Look

✳ Read Luke 8:11-15. What happens to God's Word? Which illustration best describes you today?

_____

_____

In the morning my prayer comes before You (Ps. 88:13).

InterACTion

Turn to Psalm 63 in the Bible. Read it. Think about it. Choose a verse to write and remember. Select verses to pray to God.

Day 5: Practice the Holiness Habits of Prayer and Praise

Prayer may be the most talked about and the least practiced of all Christian disciplines.

☀ **Do you agree or disagree with this statement?**
☐ Agree ☐ Disagree

When you hear prayer requests at church or someone asks you to pray, do you? ☐ Yes ☐ No

When? ☐ Right then ☐ Later ☐ Both

How often?_____

☀ **On the clock face in the margin, shade in the amount of time you spend praying on any given day. (Remember the clock face shows only half a day.)**

Of all the Christian disciplines, many people believe that prayer is the easiest for some yet the most difficult for others. Which is it for you? ☐ Easy ☐ Difficult *Why?*

_____

_____

Prayer is the Christian's basic tool for renewing his or her relationship with the Lord. Prayer is the language of relationship and opens the portal of intimacy between the human and the divine. Without a vital prayer life, your walk of holiness will become a one-sided attempt at human improvement. Prayer is the glue of a relationship with God and intertwines your heart with the Lord's.

Not only is prayer the language of this relationship, but God designed prayer to be the primary tool to release supernatural answers to your wishes, hopes, desires, and life's impossible or emergency situations. Although some believe that God doesn't intervene supernaturally today, the Bible overflows with commands to seek that very thing—a supernatural answer. What is a supernatural answer? When God hears and answers your prayer, you are the recipient of a purposeful change that God made happen just for you.

When you see the Lord answer your prayers time after time, your confidence in the power of prayer will increase. In fact, the more you recognize the Lord's answer, the more you will be encouraged to pray for hundreds of things you would never have thought of asking God to provide for you.

People today who say they pray and their prayers are never answered may not be walking in an intimate relationship with God. Many of the New Testament promises stating that God will hear and answer prayer are conditional. They depend on the pray-er's right relationship with God.

The Lord actually commands Christians to pray to Him for answers so He can give them and cause joy literally to overflow. God wants to give good gifts to His children.

And whatever things you ask in prayer, believing, you will receive (Matt. 21:22).

If you abide in Me, and My words abide in you, you will ask what you desire, and it shall be done for you (John 15:7).

The effective, fervent prayer of a righteous man avails much (Jas. 5:16).

✳ **When was the last time you knew God answered your prayer? What was your request? How did He answer?**

The Lord ... hears the prayer of the righteous (Prov. 15:29).

Daniel ... knelt down on his knees three times that day, and prayed and gave thanks before his God, as was his custom since early days (Dan. 6:10).

If you want to improve your prayer life, make it another holy habit. Giving a routine to your prayer life will ensure that you make time for prayer each day rather than allow a token few minutes to turn your heart toward God as you fall asleep each night.

Once you make prayer a part of your daily quiet time with God, the next step is knowing what to pray. If you don't establish that ahead of time, you will likely not talk with God about everything you intended.

When you pray, does your mind wander? This is not unusual. One way to overcome that is to develop a prayer list. Following is a list from *Personal Holiness in Times of Temptation* that will keep you focused on communicating with God. It includes categories you may wish to select to be a part of your prayer time. Don't add them all at once. Add those you select gradually, perhaps three or four each week until you have added all you selected.

And I prayed to the Lord my God, and made confession, and said, "O Lord, great and awesome God, who keeps His covenant and mercy with those who love Him, and with those who keep His commandments, we have sinned and committed iniquity, we have done wickedly and rebelled, even by departing from Your precepts and Your judgments" (Dan. 9:4-5).

1. *Sin.* Confess all known sin and quietly wait before the Lord, making sure your heart is clean before Him.
2. *Self.* Confess your independent nature. Humble yourself before God. Present yourself to Him as a living sacrifice. Offer your body for His use each day.
3. *Specific prayers.* Make concrete requests that you'll know for sure when God answers yes or no.

Likewise the Spirit also helps in our weaknesses. For we do not know what we should pray for as we ought, but the spirit Himself makes intercession for us with groanings which cannot be uttered (Rom. 8:26).

4. *Spirit of God.* Ask the Holy Spirit to fill you for service this day. Depend on Him for guidance, wisdom, strength, and leadership.
5. *Spiritual gifts.* Thank God for the gifts He has given you. Ask God to deepen each of those gifts. Name them. Ask Him to cleanse you from pride or selfish ambition regarding these gifts. Ask the Lord to help you narrow the focus of your life so you focus more on using those gifts for His glory.
6. *Spiritual vision.* Ask God for His vision for your life, your marriage, your family, and the places you serve Him, including your church.
7. *Spiritual service.* Pray specifically about your major responsibilities, meetings, and decisions.
8. *Spiritual warfare.* Recommit to stand and resist Satan's power. Ask God to keep you away from temptation. Precommit to choose obedience to Him.
9. *Spiritual strongholds.* Renew your mind by confessing all known unbiblical thoughts and actions. Ask God to shower His mercy and grace on you and work deeply in you.
10. *Spiritual wisdom.* Ask for the mind of Christ and His thoughts for the challenges of the day. Ask for financial stewardship and generosity. Ask for wisdom from God.
11. *Spiritual thanksgiving.* Name at least 10 specific things you're thankful for since yesterday. Rejoice with gratitude to God.
12. *Spiritual goals.* Pray for each major goal for the year. Ask for God's wisdom, patience, grace, and empowerment.
13. *Spiritual intercession.* Pray for each member of your family, extended family members, coworkers, church friends, people who don't yet know the Lord, your pastor and other Christian leaders, government leaders, and people you are mentoring.
14. *Sanctification.* Pray that you will become more like Christ.

Be anxious for nothing, but in everything by prayer and supplication, with thanksgiving, let your requests be made known to God (Phil. 4:6).

☀ **Circle the numbers of those items you'd like to add to your daily prayer time. List them below in the order you'd like to add them.**

_____

_____

_____

_____

Worship: to regard with great or extravagant respect, honor, or devotion

Praise: to glorify by attributing perfections

When do you worship? On Sunday? Is worship a part of your daily quiet time? Does your worship include praising God? Having habits is good, but having meaningless habits is not good. Attending worship service can become so much a part of our routine, and our worship services can become so predictable, that we go through the motions without ever actually worshiping God. When habits become meaningless, God despises our worship.

Praise and worship generally don't occur unless we are already walking close to God, spending time with Him daily. That close fellowship with God prompts believers to want to praise and worship the God of their salvation.

Here are some tips for including praise in your daily time with God.

1. Express to the Lord that He is worthy. Recognize and acknowledge His greatness and power.

2. Seek to connect with the Lord so personally and directly that you are unaware of other people or things. Even in public worship, your relationship with God is one-on-one.

3. Praise in singing takes place when the focus is on God. Don't allow the tempo, volume, singer, or director to distract you from letting the words focus on God.

God is worthy to be praised. Here are a few reasons Christians have to praise God.

1. Creation. Look for God's handiwork in nature each day.

2. Compassions of the Lord. How has God been merciful to you? Remember to praise for His acts of compassion.

3. Character. As you know God better, you will become increasingly aware of his characteristics. Begin by praising God for His faithfulness.

I will bless the Lord at all times; His praise shall continually be in my mouth (Ps. 34:1).

Every day I will bless You, And I will praise Your name forever and ever. Great is the Lord, and greatly to be praised; And His greatness is unsearchable (Ps. 145:2-3).

I will praise You, for I am fearfully and wonderfully made; Marvelous are Your works, And that my soul knows very well (Ps. 139:14).

☀ **Select one of the three areas above. List three attributes of that area. Praise God for the items you list. Name each one.**

1. _____

2. _____

3. _____

A Deeper Look

☀ **Jesus modeled spending time alone with God. The Gospels record times Jesus separated Himself from the crowds and went off to pray alone. Read Matthew 14:23; 26:36; and Luke 5:16; 6:12. List below other instances you remember.**

_____

_____

**Spiritual Breakthroughs
I Experienced in
My Life This Week**

_____

_____

_____

_____

_____

_____

_____

_____

_____

_____

_____

_____

InterACTion

How do you know if your prayers are answered? Many people who are serious about their prayer life keep a journal. Experiment with your design, but definitely include these items:

1. A numbering system so that you can quickly find a specific prayer.
2. A place for your request.
3. The date the prayer was asked.
4. The date you received an answer.
5. The answer.

Design your own notebook with these headings. Get started today!

---

[1] A number of devotional guides and plans are available from LifeWay Christian Resources. For more information on selecting or ordering these guides, write Customer Service Center, MSN 113; 127 Ninth Avenue, North; Nashville, TN 37234-0113; call (800) 458-2772; fax (615) 251-5933; order online at *www.lifeway.com*; email *customerservice@lifeway.com*; or visit a LifeWay Christian Store.

FINAL CHALLENGE

You've completed the journey through *The Three Chairs: Experiencing Spiritual Breakthroughs*. To complete your reflection and commitment to being a first-chair Christian, turn to the pages where you recorded your spiritual breakthroughs (pages 31, 55, 83, and 104). Read and reflect on what you have experienced. But don't let it end with this study. Continue to build on what God has done and is doing in your life. Experience spiritual breakthroughs each day with God as you sit in the first-chair in every area of your life.

Group Leader Guide

Unlike most studies, each chapter of this book can be studied either independently or consecutively. All adults—men, women, married couples, couples with children, grandparents, single adults, and single parents—can benefit from this study.

Chapter 1, "Experiencing Spiritual Breakthroughs in Your Life," is for everyone and is foundational for the other chapters. Some groups may elect not to study every chapter, but everyone should study the first chapter.

Chapter 2, "Experiencing Spiritual Breakthroughs in Your Marriage," focuses on the relationship between husband and wife. Couples who have been married for any length of time will benefit from this chapter as will young adults anticipating marriage.

Chapter 3, "Experiencing Spiritual Breakthroughs in Your Family," focuses on families with children. It is generally targeted for parents of children living at home though parents with children of any age, including grandchildren, will benefit. Childless adults who work with preschoolers, children, or youth will also benefit from this chapter.

Chapter 4, "Experiencing Spiritual Breakthroughs with God," is targeted to all believers and brings practical guidance to a close walk with God.

Select a time to meet that fits participants' schedules. Each group session takes a minimum of one hour. If the entire book is studied, participants will meet for six weeks. If your group will not use all the material, remember to plan an introductory session and a closing session, adapting other session plans to meet the needs of your group. The rule of thumb is to conduct two more sessions than the number of chapters studied.

Maintain small groups of 10 to 12 people. If you have a large viewing audience, divide into small groups for debriefing and discussion.

Groups can meet in homes or at the church, wherever a TV/VCR or video monitor is available in a quiet, comfortable place.

Promote the study using the promotional segments on the videotape. Consider showing the drama segments in large group settings (worship service, adult department) to introduce the study.

Before beginning a group study, read the entire leader guide. Each week ...
- Pray for each group member and for your role in leading as God directs.
- Check the TV/VCR to make sure it is working. Watch the entire video so you are familiar with the material when the group views it.
- Complete the workbook chapter yourself each week.
- Contact absentees and encourage everyone to participate.

SESSION 1: INTRODUCTORY SESSION

The first group session is a time for distributing workbooks, introducing the three chairs concept, and providing time for participants to get acquainted

Before the Session
1. Arrange the room so that everyone can see comfortably.
2. Place three chairs in front of the room facing the group. If possible, use three different kinds of chairs. For example, a rocker, a director's chair, and a lawn chair.
3. Set up a TV/VCR and cue the videotape so it is ready to use.
4. Provide name tags, paper, and pencils for all participants. If possible, cut out name tags shaped like chairs or decorated with chair stickers.

During the Session
1. Introduce yourself as participants arrive. Ask each person to wear a name tag. Name tags will help you call people by name and make newcomers feel included.
2. Begin on time. Introduce yourself.
3. Distribute paper and pencils. Ask participants to draw a picture of a chair that is or has been a personal favorite.
4. If the group is small, let each participant introduce himself or herself, show the drawing, and tell why that chair is a favorite. If the group is large, share in smaller groups of five or six. Tell small groups to select one member to share with the large group.
5. Comment on the variety of chairs. Display the pictures throughout the session.
6. Show the promotional segment on the videotape.
7. Say: Three chairs are the focus of all of our sessions. (Stand behind each chair as you talk about it.) The first chair represents a close walk

and fellowship with Jesus Christ. Those who sit in this chair have chosen an active, dynamic relationship with God through Christ.

The second chair also represents those who have made a profession of faith in Christ. Though they call Him Savior, they do not live accordingly.

The third chair represents persons who have not yet accepted Christ as Savior.

Those who sit in the first and second chairs can have spiritual breakthroughs in their relationship with Christ. Those sitting in the third chair can only achieve a breakthrough by first accepting Christ as Savior.

Those who sit in the first chair one week—in one area—may or may not sit there another week. You may have a close personal walk with God but still not be in the first chair as a spouse or parent. Whether you sit in the first or second chair, you will be challenged.
8. Distribute workbooks. Say: Each chapter has studies for five days. You can choose which 5 days of the week work best for you. Each chapter includes Bible study, prayer, and reflection. Allow 30 minutes to 1 hour for each day. Each day ends with two activities: Bible study and action. Do both if you sincerely want to achieve a spiritual breakthrough.

Allow participants time to look through their workbooks. Suggest that they write their names in the front of their workbooks. Say: You will benefit most if you are honest before God in answering all questions. You will not be expected to share personal details in group sessions. Do you have any questions about the workbook?
9. Encourage members to bring their workbooks and Bibles every week.
10. Invite participants to share prayer concerns. Close in prayer, voice the requests shared, and pray for participants to have spiritual breakthroughs.

SESSION 2: EXPERIENCING SPIRITUAL BREAKTHROUGHS IN YOUR LIFE

Before the Session

1. Set up three chairs and a TV/VCR. Cue the videotape.

2. Provide paper and pencils.

3. Provide extra Bibles. Bring several translations. (The workbook uses the *New King James Version* of the Bible.)

4. Duplicate copies of the audiotape in the Leader Kit for each participant.

During the Session

1. Greet participants as they arrive.

2. Begin on time. Ask participants if they have reports on prayer requests from the previous week. Ask: Which prayers have been answered?

3. Ask: Who are your biblical heroes? Why? As heroes are named, list them on a board or flip chart. If the group does not include Joshua, Abraham, David, Jesus, or Paul, mention those.

4. Explain: Biblical heroes provide real-life examples of men and women who sat in the first chair—who had firsthand faith, close relationships with God.

5. Ask: Who has modeled firsthand faith for you— a parent or another relative, a pastor, a teacher, a deacon, etc.? Allow several to share their stories.

6. Explain that today's video addresses ways we pass our faith to the generations that follow us. We will see that some biblical heroes did that better than others.

7. Show the video. Encourage participants to take notes in their workbook beginning on page 6.

8. Following the video, ask participants if they have questions or comments.

9. Ask for prayer requests. Encourage participants to pray for one another. Pray for the concerns voiced and for participants to experience spiritual breakthroughs.

10. Remind everyone to complete their work on chapter 1 (pages 10-31) before the next group meeting.

11. Provide copies of the audiotape and explain what it contains. Encourage participants to listen each day to the illustration from Bruce Wilkinson.

12. Announce the date, time, and place for the next meeting.

SESSION 3: EXPERIENCING SPIRITUAL BREAKTHROUGHS IN YOUR MARRIAGE

Before the Session

1. Set up the three chairs and the TV/VCR with the videotape cued.

2. If possible, have three large tables in the room. Each should have paper and pencils, large sheets of paper, markers, and masking tape. Label the tables: First Chair, Second Chair, Third Chair.

3. Print instructions for each table:

Instructions: Write a profile of a person in the chair assigned to your group. Describe his or her family life, characteristics about this person's relationship with God, and biblical examples.

4. Make a poster of Joshua 24:15 and display it on a focal wall in the room.

During the Session

1. As people arrive, greet them and send them to one of the three tables. Ask participants to begin discussing their "chair" as soon as each table has at least two people. Suggest that they take notes and then decide what to write on the sheets of paper once everyone has arrived.

2. Allow 10 minutes for groups to complete their work. Display the sheets and ask each group to report. At the end of each report, allow time for questions or personal testimony.

3. Ask: Does anyone have a spiritual breakthrough to share that resulted from your study? If no one responds, briefly share your experience. Then invite the group to share. Allow time for response.

4. Read together Joshua 24:15. Ask if anyone has memorized it. Read it in another translation.

5. This week's video contains sensitive material that may prompt questions and discussion. Some of their issues may be addressed in their workbook study during the week.

Say: The video tonight focuses on the roles, responsibilities, and relationship of husbands and wives based on Scripture. If you have discovered that you sit in the first chair, don't assume that you sit in the first chair in your marriage relationship. Watch and listen closely as we learn about three chairs in a marriage. Take notes in your workbook beginning on page 32. And make notes of any questions you might have for our group. We'll discuss those at our next session.

6. After the video, encourage participants to use the audiotape during their daily study this week. Announce the time and place for the next group session.

7. Say: Turn to a neighbor and share a prayer concern. If you have discovered spiritual needs in your life as a result of your study, ask for prayer without revealing anything specific. After you have prayed together, feel free to leave.

SESSION 4: EXPERIENCING SPIRITUAL BREAKTHROUGHS IN YOUR FAMILY

Before the Session
1. Set up the three chairs and the TV/VCR with the videotape cued.
2. Provide paper and pens or pencils for three small groups.
3. Provide space for three small groups. If additional rooms are available, use them.
4. Provide the following instructions for each group.

Write a script for a couple in the chair assigned to your group. Include situations that model roles, responsibilities, and relationships. Your one-act play can be high drama or comedy. Select two members to act out the play.

5. Print Genesis 2:24 on a large sheet of paper and cover it before the group arrives.

During the Session
1. Greet participants as they arrive.
2. Begin on time. Ask if anyone memorized Genesis 2:24 this week. If so, allow him or her to say it. Uncover the verse and read it together.
3. Divide participants into three groups, each containing both men and women. Husbands and wives do not have to be in the same group. This activity will work best if each group has a few extroverts.
4. Assign each group the first, second, or third chair. Give them their instructions and 10 minutes to prepare. Encourage them to have fun with this activity.

5. Call participants together. Allow all three groups to perform without comment or discussion.
6. Ask everyone to brainstorm issues raised by the dramas. Allow discussion as time permits. Not everyone will agree on the issues raised. Affirm everyone without labeling comments. Use such remarks as: "Thanks for sharing that thought." "That's a different perspective."
7. Close the discussion by focusing on the concept of choice. Allow participants to ask any remaining questions.
8. Introduce the video. Say: Next we will look at the three chairs as they relate to families, especially the role of parents. Although the focus is on parents, this will apply to those anticipating having children in the future, grandparents, and even those who work with children. Encourage participants to take notes in the workbook beginning on page 56.
9. After the video, ask participants if they have questions or comments.
10. Tell participants to make sure they bring their Bibles the following week. Encourage them to continue using the audiotape during their daily study.
11. Ask participants if they have prayer requests about family members. Pray, addressing specific requests, thanking God for families, and asking for spiritual breakthroughs in group members' lives.
12. As you dismiss, announce the date, time, and place of the next group session.

SESSION 5: EXPERIENCING SPIRITUAL BREAKTHROUGHS WITH GOD

Before the Session

1. Set up the three chairs and the TV/VCR with the videotape cued.

2. Have several extra Bibles on hand.

3. Prepare questions for a contest about the Word and works of God. Make your own questions or use a Bible trivia game or book. Here are suggestions to get you started.

- How many books are in the Old Testament? (39) the New Testament? (27)
- Name the types of writing found in the Old Testament (law, history, poetry, major prophets, minor prophets).
- Name the types of writing found in the New Testament (Gospels, history, Paul's letters, general letters, prophecy).
- In what book do you find the story of creation? (Genesis)
- In what book do you find the Ten Commandments? (Exodus)
- Which book has songs written by David? (Psalms)
- What is the last book in the Old Testament? (Malachi)
- Which book tells about the early church? (Acts)
- Which book records the life of Abraham? (Genesis)
- In which Gospels will you find the Lord's Prayer? (Luke and Matthew)
- What book tells about a virtuous woman? (Proverbs)
- Which Gospels record the Sermon on the Mount? (Matthew, Luke)
- In which Gospel does Jesus meet with Nicodemus? (John)
- Which book is often used in the plan of salvation? (Romans)
- What are the five books of Law? (Genesis, Exodus, Leviticus, Numbers, Deuteronomy)
- Which book does not include a reference to God? (Esther)
- Which book is about one man's suffering? (Job)
- Which of Paul's letters were written to an individual? (1 and 2 Timothy)

5. Print Deuteronomy 6:6-7 on a large sheet of paper and display it.

During the Session

1. Greet participants as they arrive.

2. Ask if anyone has comments or questions about their study this past week. Allow several to share.

3. Divide participants into three equal teams. Ask participants to arrange their chairs in groups where everyone can see you. Facilitate a contest about the Word and works of God. You ask a question. Participants stand when they have the answer. Call on the first person who stands. Keep score. Award five points for multi-part questions and one point for questions with one part. Award no points for incorrect answers. If participants are enjoying the game, follow the questions with a Bible drill, using verses from the workbook. Congratulate winners.

4. Invite members to share breakthroughs they had this week.

5. Ask people to gather in small groups of three to five of the same gender. Ask them to tell one another about their families: number of children, ages, interests, etc. Then ask them to share prayer requests about each child. Invite those without children to share about nieces/nephews, a close friend's child, or just listen.

6. Say: The last video is about ways we can have a closer walk with God. Encourage participants to take notes in the workbook beginning on page 84.

7. After the video, ask participants if they have questions or comments.

8. Read together Deuteronomy 6:6-7. Ask the small groups who shared about their families to pray together for the children named.

9. As you dismiss, encourage members to attend the final group session.

SESSION 6: CLOSING SESSION

Before the Session

1. Set up the three chairs.

2. If possible, provide a gift for each participant. The gift may be a symbol to wear—t-shirt, bracelet, small pin—or something for their office or home—mug, calendar. The gift should clearly identify the user/wearer as a Christian. The gift may include the name of your church or *WWJD?*, for example.

3. Prepare copies of Psalm 63:1-8 and Psalm 150 for each participant. Prepare Psalm 63:1-8 as a responsive reading.

4. Have an adequate amount of large sheets of paper and markers.

During the Session

1. Begin on time. Remind participants that this is the final session.

2. Ask: What Scripture verses have become meaningful to you during the past few weeks. Write the Scripture references on a large sheet of paper.

3. Distribute copies of Psalm 63:1-8. Pray this Psalm back to God responsively, alternating verses between men and women.

4. Ask: What words and their definitions have taken on new meaning to you? Write the words where everyone can see them. Discuss each word mentioned.

5. Ask: What hinders people in the second chair from moving to the first chair? Be prepared to answer if responses are not forthcoming. Responses can come from any chapter or group session.

6. Read 2 Chronicles 7:14. Pray that God will give those who seek Him the courage to humble themselves, pray to God in repentance, abandon their sins, and walk closer with God.

7. Ask: How can we draw closer to God.? List and discuss these. Ask: Why do we sometimes fail in doing the very things we know will draw us closer to God?

8. Ask volunteers who have had a breakthrough to take turns coming to the front and sitting in the first chair. Tell them they do not need to explain their breakthrough if they do not feel comfortable doing so, but simply say, *I've had a spiritual breakthrough in my walk with God.* Or, *I've had a breakthrough as a parent or a spouse.*

9. Pray for the group, that all will continue to walk in fellowship with Jesus Christ and have an increasingly intimate relationship with Him.

10. Distribute the gifts. Turn the tone from serious to celebrative.

11. Hand out copies of Psalm 150. Lead the group in saying it together as a closing praise to God.

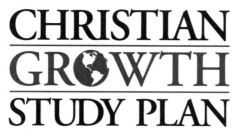

CHRISTIAN GROWTH STUDY PLAN

Preparing Christians to Serve

In the **Christian Growth Study Plan (formerly Church Study Course)**, *The Three Chairs: Experiencing Spiritual Breakthroughs* is a resource for course credit the subject area Personal Life in the Christian Growth category of diploma plans. To receive credit, read the book; complete the learning activities; attend group sessions; show your work to your pastor, a staff member or a church leader; then complete the following information. This page may be duplicated. Send the completed page to:

Christian Growth Study Plan
127 Ninth Avenue, North, MSN 117
Nashville, TN 37234-0117
FAX: (615)251-5067

For information about the Christian Growth Study Plan, refer to the current Christian Growth Study Plan Catalog. Your church office may have a copy. If not, request a free copy from the Christian Growth Study Plan office (615/251-2525).

The Three Chairs
COURSE NUMBER: CG-0524

Social Security Number (USA ONLY)	Personal CGSP Number*	Date of Birth (MONTH, DAY, YEAR)

Name (First, Middle, Last)		Home Phone

Address (Street, Route, or P.O. Box)	City, State, or Province	Zip/Postal Code

CHURCH INFORMATION

Church Name

Address (Street, Route, or P.O. Box)	City, State, or Province	Zip/Postal Code

CHANGE REQUEST ONLY

☐ Former Name

☐ Former Address	City, State, or Province	Zip/Postal Code

☐ Former Church	City, State, or Province	Zip/Postal Code

Signature of Pastor, Conference Leader, or Other Church Leader	Date

*New participants are requested but not required to give SS# and date of birth. Existing participants, please give CGSP# when using SS# for the first time. Thereafter, only one ID# is required. **Mail to:** Christian Growth Study Plan, 127 Ninth Ave., North, Nashville, TN 37234-0117. Fax: (615)251-5067

Rev. 6-99